Jacob August Otto, John Bishop

A treatise on the structure and preservation of the violin and all other bow-instruments

Together with an account of the most celebrated makers, and of the genuine

characteristics of their instruments

Jacob August Otto, John Bishop

A treatise on the structure and preservation of the violin and all other bow-instruments
Together with an account of the most celebrated makers, and of the genuine characteristics of their instruments

ISBN/EAN: 9783743357402

Hergestellt in Europa, USA, Kanada, Australien, Japan

Cover: Foto ©Thomas Meinert / pixelio.de

Manufactured and distributed by brebook publishing software (www.brebook.com)

Jacob August Otto, John Bishop

A treatise on the structure and preservation of the violin and all

other bow-instruments

A TREATISE

ON THE

STRUCTURE AND PRESERVATION

OF THE

VIOLIN

AND ALL OTHER BOW-INSTRUMENTS;

TOGETHER WITH AN ACCOUNT OF   Ġ

THE MOST CELEBRATED MAKERS,

AND OF THE GENUINE CHARACTERISTICS OF THEIR INSTRUMENTS;

BY

JACOB AUGUSTUS OTTO,

INSTRUMENT MAKER TO THE COURT OF THE GRAND DUKE OF WEIMAR.

———

TRANSLATED FROM THE ORIGINAL, WITH ADDITIONS AND ILLUSTRATIONS.

BY

JOHN BISHOP,

OF CHELTENHAM.

———

FOURTH EDITION : FURTHER ENLARGED

LONDON:
WILLIAM REEVES

AUTHOR'S PREFACE.

In the present age, Music forms one of the favourite occupations of polished society, and frequently affords the highest gratification, as well in the small domestic circle as in large assemblies. Parents of cultivated minds often expend much money in providing their children with a talented musical instructor, and spare no expense in the purchase of an instrument: but, unless possessed of sufficient knowledge to guide them, they are often exposed to gross imposition, as I have frequently observed in repairing instruments. Many parents, for instance, have given from six to ten pistoles for a violin which was scarcely worth as many dollars.

In consideration of this, and as it is but reasonable to suppose that a man must be thoroughly acquainted with the business which he follows, I have been induced to draw up a minute description of the construction of the violin and all other bow-instruments, together with a careful explanation of the forms of the genuine Italian instruments, by which they may be clearly distinguished from the spurious imitations. I shall specify those makers who, next to the Cremonese, have produced the best instruments, and worked on the most correct mathematical principles, and shall treat at large of the rules which should be observed in repairing; because, through this,

most of the good Italian violins, and those of other celebrated makers, have been spoiled.

Having been engaged for the last thirty years in the
restoration of such damaged instruments, and in the construction of new ones ; and having, from my youth, studied
music, mathematics, physics and acoustics, I consider
myself better qualified to reason on this Art, with the
practical experience gained during the above period, than
one who merely understands the subject theoretically, or
who only imitates the work of another without thinking
for himself.   Daily experience proves, that even many
renowned instrument-makers fall into error in this respect;
and I imagine that I shall not be bestowing an unacceptable
service on many reflecting performers and lovers of music,
in directing their attention to the best means of preserving
a good instrument, and of improving a damaged one. The
assurance of having produced a work of any real utility,
would amply reward me for my labour.

TRANSLATOR'S PREFACE.

———•———

THE favourable reception accorded to the first edition of this translation having occasioned a demand for a second, I have sought to render it still more interesting to the violinist, and to musical readers generally, by the addition of numerous particulars, inserted either in foot notes or in the Appendix, and culled from a variety of works and detached articles on the subject of this treatise; most of which, having been published either in French or German, were unlikely to come under the notice of English musicians.

But, in the whole range of musical literature, perhaps no works are so indifferently viewed, and even decried, as those which treat of the construction of musical instruments. It is true this chiefly proceeds from the very persons for whom such works are not intended—the makers or repairers of the respective instruments; though even many professors and amateurs fall into a similar erroneous estimate of such books, either because the particulars found in them do not suffice to make them manufacturers, or because such particulars chance to differ from some previous knowledge which they possess.

As regards the former objection, it may be confidently answered, that books alone cannot possibly fulfil such expectations; and, as to the latter, it is a well-known fact that different workmen, as well as different establishments, frequently proceed in a dissimilar manner in the construction of the several parts of musical instruments, which, when finished, may and do assume pretty much the same appearance.

Hence it follows that most works of this description must be necessarily regarded in a liberal spirit, as merely tending to diffuse a *general*—not *specific*—acquaintance, among musicians and others, with the subjects on which they treat; and, if they succeed so far, they evidently accomplish their purpose.

———

In preparing this new edition, besides the introduction of many interesting particulars drawn from the most modern works on the subject, I had the advantage of consulting Mr. George Chanot, the well-known violin maker of Wardour Street, London, (and nephew of the ingenious French officer mentioned at page 72).

JOHN BISHOP

CONTENTS.

A TREATISE ON THE VIOLIN.

CHAPTER I.

ON THE CONSTRUCTION OF THE VIOLIN AND OTHER BOW-INSTRUMENTS.

OF all instruments played with a bow, the Violin is doubtless that which enjoys the greatest share of popularity, and which is most admired. I shall therefore commence by describing it, particularly as the Tenor, Violoncello, and Double-bass are likewise composed of the same parts.

When in a state fit for use, the violin consists of fifty-eight distinct parts ; namely :

2 pieces for the back.	†1 piece for the tail-piece.
2 —— for the belly.	4 —— pegs.
6 —— blocks at the top, bottom, and four corners.	1 —— nut. [piece.
	1 —— button for the tail-
6 —— sides.	4 —— strings.
12 —— lining for the sides.	1 —— catgut or wire to con-
1 —— bass-bar.	nect the tail-piece
'12 —— purfling.	with the button.
1 —— rest for tail-piece.	1 —— sound-post.
1 —— neck.	1 —— bridge.
1 —— finger-board.	Total 58 pieces.

---

* The *Manuel de Musique*, by Choron and Lafage, and the *Manuel du Luthier*, by Maugin, give 24 pieces for the purfling. When, however, the strips of wood forming this ornament are three in number, and joined at the top and bottom of the back and belly on the line formed by the middle joint of those parts, instead of being carried round from corner to corner, as many as 36 pieces are employed. But some authors mention only two strips for the purfling, in which case the number of pieces would again be reduced to 24. See Welcker von Gontershausen's *Neu eröffnetes Magazin musikalischer Tonwerkzeuge* (Frankfort a. M., 1855), p. 207.—*Tr.*

† The tail-piece sometimes consists of 2 pieces. See the first two works named in the preceding note.—*Tr.*

Now, though all these are not indispensably necessary—since, in common instruments, the side-linings as well as the corner-blocks are often omitted, and occasionally, in good violins, the back or the belly is worked out of a single piece, instead of two glued together, and sometimes even both are so formed—still, it may be received as a general rule, that a complete violin consists of the fifty-eight parts which we have enumerated ; a fact, indeed, which is evident from the very construction of the instrument, and which therefore admits of no doubt.

A violin is usually made of three kinds of wood : the back, neck, sides, side-linings,* and bridge, consisting of maple ; the belly,† bass-bar, sound-post, and six blocks, of pine or white deal ; and the finger-board and tail-piece of ebony.‡ The wood for the belly, as being of the utmost importance for the production of a good tone, should be cut in the month of December or January, and only the south-side of the tree used. This must be split in such a manner as to leave each piece an inch thick at the bark-side, and a quarter of an inch at the heart of the tree. Maple for the back must be cut in a similar way, but the whole of the tree

---

* Other authors name pine or deal as the wood generally used for the *side-linings*. Otto himself, in a more recent edition of his work, says they are made of nut-tree, maple, or pine, and the blocks of pine or lime wood.—*Tr.*

† The Abbé Sibire, in *La Chélonomie, ou le parfait Luthier* (Paris, 1806), the anonymous author of *Luthomonographie* (Munich, 1856), and Savart, in his *Mémoire sur la construction des instruments à cordes et à archet* (Paris, 1819), mention cedar as having also been used for the belly ; but this must be considered exceptional.—*Tr.*

‡ Gavin Wilson, of Edinburgh, made a violin of leather, hardened, said to be "not inferior to any constructed of wood." (*Gentleman's Magazine*, LXXXIII., p. 312. 1813.) Violins have also been made in silver, copper, and brass, but have proved weak and disagreeable in tone. (Leipzig *Allgem. Mus. Zeitung*, VII., p. 50. 1804.)—*Tr.*

may be used, the pieces when cut measuring six inches in breadth.

After the wood thus prepared has been exposed to the air for five or six years (but not to the sun or rain), it may be employed in the manufacture of violins.*   For this purpose,

---

* Since the publication of the first German edition of this work, several artificial means have been employed in order to prepare the wood for the manufacture of violins, &c.   Thus, in the Leipzig *Allgemeine musikalische Zeitung* for 1839, p. 1046, Schlick is mentioned as having discovered a process (not described) for depriving wood of the water, acid, resin, &c., which it contains, by which means he was enabled to make violins with a tone scarcely distinguishable from that of the best old Italian instruments ; and in the *Bulletin* for 1822, issued by the Paris Society for the Encouragement of National Industry, it is stated that an establishment was then formed at Vienna for preparing wood intended to make musical instruments, &c., by steaming it in a room or chest 10 feet by 5, made of strong boards, well joined.   " This steam, by penetrating the pores of the wood, softens the vegetable parts, and renders them susceptible of being dissolved.   The steam condensed in the chest forms, in the lower part, a liquor at first but slightly coloured, which becomes deeper as the operation proceeds ; at length it is quite clear, and acquires a very decided acid taste.   This is let off by a proper pipe.   The operation commonly lasts 60 hours.   The wood is afterwards taken out and dried in a stove heated to 42° or 48° Reaumur (= 126½° or 140° Fahrenheit).   The dessication lasts two or three days, when the boards are half an inch thick ; but, if thicker, several weeks, or even months, are necessary.   This wood acquires such a degree of dryness as to resist all the variations of the atmosphere ; its colour increases in intensity, particularly the wood of the walnut-tree, cherry-tree, and maple.   It becomes firmer and more sonorous, which is a great advantage for musical instruments.   Sound-boards for pianos resound much better than the common ones.   Violins also acquire the quality of the esteemed old instruments, of which the true merit is due perhaps to the slow dessication which the wood composing them has undergone."

C. A. Galbusera, who, in the year 1832, manufactured violins and tenors of a simplified form (that is, without corners—the sides being bent into a shape resembling that of a guitar, like the violins of M. Chanot ; see Note *, p. 74), is said to have previously applied to the wood he used a peculiar chemical preparation of his discovery,

the thick or bark-parts of the pieces for the belly are so
fitted and glued together, that the under side may be even,
but the upper or outside elevated down the middle and
slanting off gradually towards the edges, something like the
flat roof of a house. (See Illustrations, *Fig.* 1.) The even
side is then smoothed and the model traced on it,* after

---

for the purpose of extracting the resinous particles from it. (Leipzig
Allgem. Mus. Zeitung, XXXIV., pp. 833-4. 1832.)

The enthusiastic and ingenious Mackintosh, now deceased, published an interesting pamphlet at Dublin, in 1837, under the title of
"*Remarks on the Construction and Materials employed in the Manufacture of Violins*," in which he observes :—"I am borne out by
traditionary accounts in believing that the Cremona makers actually
put their wood through some process for the purpose of not only
preserving, but cleansing it, and making it consequently a better
conductor of sound." This cleansing refers to the extraction of the
resinous or gummy substance with which the pores of the wood are
clogged, and in effecting which, without injury to the wood itself,
the great difficulty consists. Mackintosh further states that the
wood must not only be of firm and regular texture, but have "pores
of a certain size and formation ; and, above all, it is essential that it
shall have attained, not only full maturity of growth, but shall have
remained for some years after being felled, in order to make it fit to
go through a process by which the pores (for that is the great object
to be arrived at) may be rendered so perfectly dried and cleared, as
not afterwards to be liable to close or alter their natural position, or
become crooked or irregular, as would be the inevitable consequence
if cut up immediately into thin pieces, as it is then liable to shrink,
which is also objectionable, as being injurious to the pores." He
subsequently adds—"When experimenting, I have had recourse to
steaming, steeping, stoving, boiling, and baking the timber : I have
also used all kinds of spirits, caustics, and acids ; but all these dis-
organized the pores and impaired the fibres of the timber, which
ought to be preserved in a sound and perfect state." The secret of
his own process for the thorough cleansing of the pores is not declared.
Notwithstanding what Mackintosh here says, Abele assures us, at
p. 98 of the second edition of his work, *Die Violine* (Neuburg, 1874),
there is no proof whatever in existence that the old Italians used
any artificial means for drying or preparing their wood.—*Tr.*

* A simple method of tracing a model is given in No. I. of the
Appendix.—*Tr.*

which the wood is cut and filed away on the outside ; and when the convex part is entirely finished, the inside is worked out in a similar manner : in doing this, a pair of double callipers are highly necessary, for the purpose of carefully ascertaining the thickness in every part of the belly. The *f*-holes are now cut out, and the bass-bar glued on. The back is formed precisely in the same way.

The sides, between the back and the belly, are first made perfectly straight and smooth, then bent on a hot iron, and afterwards glued, in a frame or mould, to the corner and end blocks ; the linings are then stuck to the sides above and below, and, when the whole is dry, the latter with the blocks and linings are made even, removed from the frame, and glued to the back: this being done, the belly is put on, and the purfling let into it and the back.

Lastly : the neck with the scroll is fastened with glue to the upper end block, and the finger-board, nut, pegs, tail-piece, bridge, sound-post, &c., added to the whole. The other bow-instruments are constructed and put together exactly in the same manner.*

---

* The order in which these various operations are performed does not always precisely agree with that mentioned by Otto ; but this makes no difference to the instruments when finished. — *Tr.*

CHAPTER II.

ACCOUNT OF THE MOST EMINENT GERMAN MAKERS, WHO HAVE
SO SUCCESSFULLY IMITATED THE VIOLINS OF THE CREMONESE
AND THOSE OF THE CELEBRATED *JACOB STEINER,* THAT THEIR
INSTRUMENTS CAN ONLY BE DISTINGUISHED FROM THE GENUINE
ONES BY THE MOST EXPERIENCED PERSONS.

THOSE who understand the construction of the violin may
possibly deem the previous observations superfluous ; but I
have frequently been asked, whether the back and belly
were pressed or screwed up in moulds to bring them into
the required shape ;* and this question, which shews that
many good violinists are unacquainted with the construction
and the various component parts of their instrument, has
induced me to give a minute description of them.

Musicians frequently enquire why violins are not now made
equal in quality to the old Cremonese ;† and many attribute

---

* This is now said to be done in the manufacture of common
instruments.—*Tr.*

† Welcker von Gontershausen believes that the best violins,
especially those of Germany, are as well made in the present day as
those of Amati, Stradivari, and others, when they were first turned
out of hand. Abele also thinks that, with good wood, and by
scrupulously following a good model, it is still possible to produce
as finely made instruments as formerly. (See *Die Violine*, p. 99.)
The Abbé Sibire attributes the superiority of the instruments of the
old Italian makers more to the exquisite choice of the wood used
for them, than to their age. The general opinion, however, now
entertained (as will be seen further on) is that age and careful use
combined are the chief requisites for bringing well-made instruments
to maturity.—*Tr.*

it to the negligence or unskilfulness of the present makers
and those of late years : but I dare affirm that the fault lies
principally with the musicians and amateurs themselves, for
reasons which I shall proceed to state.

All those who have sought to attain a knowledge of good
makers will, besides the Cremonese and Steiner * violins (of
which I shall afterwards particularly treat), know how to
appreciate those which have been made by *Statelmann*† of
Vienna, *Jauch*‡ of Dresden, *Withalm*‖ of Nuremberg, *Hoffmann* and *Hunger* of Leipzig, *Buchstädter* of Ratisbon, *Hassert* of Rudolstadt, *Hassert* of Eisenach, *Klotz* in the Tyrol,
Rauch of Breslau, *Rauch* of Würtzburg, *Riess* of Bamberg,
Scheinlein of Langenfeld, near Erlangen, *Fr. Ruppert* of
Erfurt, *Francis Schonger, George Schonger*, and *Bachmann*
of Berlin, *Straube* of Berlin, *Ulric Eberle* of Prague, *Charles
Helmer* of Prague, *Samuel Fritzsche* of Leipzig, *Dürfel* of
Altenburg, *Schmidt* of Cassell, and many others.

These makers have constructed their instruments with
great care and skill; and a good unspoiled violin of Statelmann, of Vienna, is preferable to the best Tyrolese, as he
used superior wood for the belly, and so admirably imitated
Jacob Steiner's violins, that his own rank next to them in
merit. After Statelmann comes Leopold Withalm, of Nuremberg, whose instruments so closely resemble Steiner's in
their exterior, that it requires a great connoisseur to distinguish them from his.

Rauch, of Breslau, has also turned out very good violins;

---

* Otto, in the more recent edition of his work (Jena, 1828), invariably spells this name *Stainer*, and modern writers also. —*Tr.*

† Sometimes spelt *Stadelmann.*—*Tr.*

‡ Spelt *Jaug* in the 1823 edition.—*Tr.*

‖ Sometimes spelt *Widhalm.*—*Tr.*

they have, however, a peculiar model, which neither resembles the Italian nor Steiner's. When unspoiled, they possess a round and powerful tone. The instruments made by his brother, at Würtzburg, are very much like them in shape and in all other respects. Both probably learned their business from the same maker. Riess, of Bamberg, has beautifully imitated Steiner, and even surpassed Rauch in quality of tone.

Scheinlein, of Langenfeld, adopted a shape peculiar to himself; but his instruments are made too weak, and hence most of them have either given way or been spoiled in repairing. He was nevertheless celebrated forty or fifty years ago, and the majority of the instruments then used in the chapels were made by him.

Buchstädter, of Ratisbon, has imitated the Cremonese makers. His instruments are rather flat than otherwise, and covered with a brown varnish. They are carefully constructed according to the principles of acoustics, and, had the bellies been made of the soft pine-wood found in Germany and Switzerland, instead of coarse-grained deal, the tone of them would have been less harsh. On this account they are not highly esteemed.

Jauch, of Dresden, has manufactured very good violins on the model of the Cremonese, and displayed, in his beautiful and excellent workmanship, a thorough knowledge of the wood, and of the due proportions of strength required in the respective parts of the instrument. But his violins produce a very weak, squally tone, when they have been carelessly repaired: though even in this case they may be often restored and brought nearly to equal the Italian, by placing them in the hands of an experienced maker, possessing a knowledge of mathematics and acoustics, without which they will be completely spoiled.

Martin Hoffmann, of Leipzig, who is chiefly known as a skilful lute-maker, has also constructed violins of an excellent quality of tone, unless that has been affected by so-called repairs ; but their size, and the form of the ƒ-holes, as well as their sharp corners and very weak edges, give his instruments such an ungraceful appearance that but few of them are esteemed by connoisseurs.

Hunger, of Leipzig, has made much more beautiful violins than Hoffmann. His tenors and violoncellos are constructed more in the Italian style, and may justly be ranked among the good German-made instruments, if their interior proportions have not been destroyed by bunglers.

Ulric Eberle, of Prague, was one of the most eminent German makers. His violins have even been mistaken by experienced connoisseurs for genuine Italian instruments, and are only inferior to the Cremonese from having a sharper or somewhat less full and round tone.

Charles Helmer, a pupil of Eberle, of Prague, has also produced very finely-made instruments. They have, however, the fault, that the three upper strings improve greatly by being played on, but the G-string, in most of them, remains so far inferior, that while the tone of the former is such as may be expected from a full-sized violin, that of the latter only resembles a child's toy-instrument. Yet an experienced maker would find no difficulty in correcting this fault.

Hassert, of Rudolstadt, has constructed his instruments with much care. They have all a very high model, and the belly is formed of excellent wood ; notwithstanding this, they produce either a shrill tone, or else, when weakly made, a hollow one. His brother, at Eisenach, who far surpassed him, imitated the flat model of the Italians with great assiduity, and used very beautiful wood for the bellies of his instruments, many of which have been mistaken for Italian by inexperienced judges.

Ruppert, of Erfurt, had a model and system of construction peculiar to himself. His violins, tenors, and violoncellos are very flat, and have a powerful tone ; but they are slightly put together, for the sides are not lined, and the corner blocks are omitted. Nevertheless his instruments are still prized, on account of the excellent construction of the belly and the back, the correct proportions of thickness observed in them, and also for their good tone ; though they are not even purfled, and have a dark brown amber varnish, and nothing recommendatory in their exterior.

Francis Schonger, of Erfurt, has made many high-modelled instruments, which are much more beautiful in appearance than Ruppert's ; but they are, throughout, extremely weak in the wood, and have a dull, hollow tone. Connoisseurs therefore consider them greatly inferior to Ruppert's.

George Schonger, of Erfurt, abandoned his father's system of construction, and imitated the Italian style. Excellent instruments exist of his make, which are particularly distinguished for their accurate arrangement (*Aptirung**). He was greatly renowned, in his time, as a repairer of the good old instruments.

---

* Here, and in two other places in this work, I have viewed the word "*Aptirung*" as synonymous with "*Einrichtung*" [*arrangement—adjustment—fitting up*] as used by Spohr; who says, in his Violin School), Part I., Sec. 2.—"By the arrangement (Einrichtung) of the violin is meant—first, the position of the neck and finger-board, the height of the bridge and that of the strings above the finger-board, with regard to the convenience of playing ; and, secondly, the situation of the bridge and sound-post, their strength and height, as also the choice of wood for them, with reference to the tone of the instrument." (See the translator's edition of Spohr's School, published by Messrs. Cocks and Co.)—*Tr.*

Bachmann, of Berlin, was one of the most celebrated German makers ; and, as his instruments have already attained a considerable age, they rank next in point of quality to the Cremonese. They are very correct in their proportions, and, though made rather too strong than otherwise, wood of the best quality has been used for them ; so that one of his violins is even preferable to a Cremonese which has fallen into unskilful hands, such as I shall describe at length in treating of the rules to be observed in repairing.

Straube, of Berlin, was also an excellent workman. I have seen only a few of his instruments, but those were very good. From his constant occupation in repairing old instruments, he has probably not made many new ones.

Schmidt, of Cassel, has, at the present day (1817), made some very beautiful violins in imitation of those by Straduarius, which in process of time may become excellent, if they do not get spoiled before they arrive at their best.*

Dürfel, of Altenburg, was one of those makers, who,

---

* The following additional particulars of this maker are given in the more recent German edition :—

"Besides Bachmann, Schmidt, of Cassell, has perhaps most successfully approached his model. His instruments, it is true, are not altogether satisfactory in their construction, but they can easily be brought into correct proportions. Owing to their illusive similarity, many of his old instruments have already been sold under the name of Straduarius. Although fine in the wood, they are still cognizable ; the back not being made of such finely-figured maple, and the wood of the belly (from the upper Hercynian forest) not being quite equal in the grain. Most of them have, from the middle joint, an inch or an inch and a half of fine grained wood ; then about an inch of coarse ; and so on alternately for the breadth of the belly. The rise of the back and belly and the form of the ƒ-holes are very well imitated ; but the edges are broader than those of Straduarius, and the purfling is set farther inwards. The scooping out, to the depth of nearly half the thickness of the edges, which is observable in the Italian instruments [within the purfling] is entirely wanting in those

without paying too great a regard to the exterior, have nevertheless turned out instruments which are excellent in point of tone. His double-basses (*Violons* *), which may be met with in most of the chapels, are particularly good, and maintain the first rank among those manufactured in Germany.

The Tyrolese makers, who carried on an extensive business, have produced a great number of violins, tenors, and violoncellos, most of which, however, have been sold under fictitious names as genuine Cremonese or Steiner's. Much deceit is practised with these instruments ; and, as no one has hitherto given an accurate description of them, cases of this kind are still of daily occurrence. The characteristics of the genuine Italian instruments will be treated of at length in the next Chapter.

Egitia Klotz was the most respectable of the Tyrolese makers, as he sent out all his instruments under his own name. They are made better than any of the violins of his countrymen ; for, instead of employing the white larch wood used by them, he manufactured the bellies of good Swiss pine : hence his instruments, which are constructed agreeably to the rules of acoustics, possess a finer and more powerful tone than any other of the Tyrolese. His son, Joseph Klotz, also sent out instruments under his own

---

of Schmidt, who also has everywhere preserved an equal height for the sides, which, in the Cremonese models, gradually diminish one-eighth of an inch in approaching the neck. The scroll is not so deep, nor so finely carved ; and lastly, instead of the excellent amber varnish used by the Italians, Schmidt has covered his instruments with spirit varnish, or merely polished them."—*Tr.*

* No "discrepancy on the part of the author" occurs here, as a former translator of this work imagined, the word *Violon* signifying. in German. a double-bass ; *not* a violin, as he supposed.—*Tr.*

name; which, as he followed his father's system, but was better acquainted with the quality of wood, are far preferable to those made by him. In their exterior arrangement (*Aptirung*), however, they all require the hand of a skilful workman; for, in the state in which he left them, they are unfit for use.

But even if these makers had worked with the same care, and possessed the same skill as we find displayed in the construction of the genuine Cremonese and Steiner's violins, still their instruments would not be equal, for the first year or two, to a Cremonese or Steiner which had been used for upwards of a century.* This would be impossible, from the very nature of the case. Many musicians and amateurs who possess good (though, certainly, not very old) instruments, have not the patience to wait until they gradually improve by use and careful treatment,† but intrust them to

---

* The *use*, and not the mere *age* of the instrument is the point here insisted on by Otto, as may be seen from a subsequent remark at p. 47; and in reference to the skill of the workman, Mackintosh, before-mentioned, declares that, by following out his theory, respecting the pores of the wood, "it is not only possible to manufacture a good violin with certainty," but by minutely attending to the instructions, as given by him, "a peculiar quality of tone can be effected," which, he says, he states from experience. Savart. too, is equally certain that excellent violins may be made by attending to the results of *his* experiments, as given in No. III. of the Appendix. If all this be true, it may serve in some measure to account for the following statement, translated from the Leipzig *Allgem. Mus. Zeitung*, XLIV., p. 380—1842 :—"The instrument-maker, Darche, of Aachen, has attracted the attention of violin judges and others in Frankfort-on-the-Maine, by a collection of old violins and some of his own manufacture. He is said to be able to imitate the old Italian violins in the most illusive manner, and in an incommunicable way to *inoculate his instruments*, as it were, *with the very character of the tone of each master he professes to follow*."—*Tr.*

† According to Abele (see *Die Violine*, p. 158), it requires from thirty to forty years' playing on a violin to bring it to perfection.—*Tr.*

bad instrument-makers or itinerant workmen. In this occupation, one Kirschschlag, and others of the same class, who could no longer prosper as musicians, travelled through most of the towns of Germany, about thirty years ago. They wished to bring in the true "*Zirkelschlag*,"* which the great Italian and German makers had neglected! But these men, whatever may have been their merit as instrumental performers, were totally unacquainted with mathematics, acoustics, or physics, and altogether inexperienced in the art of making instruments. Still, however, many people were defrauded of their money by these corrupt musical quacks or fault-finders, whose skill consisted in scraping out the wood, putting in much stronger bass-bars, and the like refinements, which threw the instruments completely out of their mathematical proportions, and entirely spoiled them. More than a hundred instances of this kind have fallen under my own observation. Even genuine Cremonese and Steiner violins have been brought to me which were ruined in this manner.

It must excite feelings of the deepest regret in all who entertain a high regard for such perfect masterpieces of art, constructed strictly according to the rules of mathematics, to witness the irreparable loss arising from such mutilation.

That the foregoing statement is not in the least exaggerated, many will have proved by their own experience; and it is further certain, that there are few towns without either a hautboy-player, fiddler, or town-musician, who

---

* By the term *Zirkelschlag*, I understand the cutting away the wood in the back and belly according to circles described on them; for further particulars of which, see Appendix, No. I., and illustrative figures. It may also include the circular arc drawn and cut out as a pattern for the convexity. See *Fig.* 2 of the illustrations.— *Tr.*

meddies with the repair and improvement of instruments, without possessing any accurate knowledge of their construction. What such men can do, may be judged of from their work! The great loss, however, which the musical public suffers through these fellows, consists in the few good instruments which exist, compared with the number which are spoiled.

One would suppose that, as the world grows wiser, such mechanics would no longer meet with encouragement; yet, even in the present day, there are people to be found who still look upon them as great artists.

CHAPTER III.

NOTICE OF THE MOST ESTEEMED ITALIAN AND *STEINER'S* VIOLINS,
WITH A DESCRIPTION OF THEIR STRUCTURE. COMPARISON
BETWEEN THESE AND THE COUNTERFEIT INSTRUMENTS.

I HAVE had about thirty Cremonese violins under my
hands, of the following makers.

The oldest were made by *Jerome Amati*, at the beginning
of the seventeenth century : after him came *Anthony Amati*,
in the middle of that century ; and, then, *Nicholas Amati*,
towards the end. *Anthony Straduarius*, of Cremona, flourished
at the end of the same century, and *Joseph Guarnerius*, at
the beginning of the eighteenth century.*

All the instruments above referred to were formed after
the simplest rules of mathematics ; and the six which I
received unspoiled were so constructed, that the belly was
thickest in the middle. where the bridge stood ; it then
diminished about one-third at the *f*-holes, and, where it
rested on the sides, it was only half as thick as in the mid
dle. The same proportion was observed in the length. The
thickness of the middle was maintained as far as the length
of the bass-bar, and then diminished one-half to the upper
and lower end blocks. The breadth was so proportioned
that the cheeks were three-fourths the thickness of the
breast ; and the edges all round, only one-half the thickness.

---

* For more exact historical details and additional particulars of
the Cremonese makers, and some others, see Appendix, No. II.—*Tr.*

These are the proportions best adapted for obtaining a full round, and sonorous tone. Whoever thinks that I should give an exact scale for the particular height, fall, and thickness of the belly, calculated in hundredth-parts of an inch, is mistaken. Such calculations I certainly make for myself; but, here, I am not writing for instrument-makers, nor for those who busy themselves with repairing, without being able to construct a violin; but simply for professors and amateurs, in order to give them a general knowledge of the correct proportions of a good instrument.

The back is formed in the same proportion as the belly, but is, in most violins, rather thicker in the wood.

During two years, I measured and calculated the proportions of the very best instruments, according to the rules of mathematics, under the late Herr Ernst, Concert-director at Gotha, with whom I also studied music for three years. Herr Ernst himself made excellent violins, as the reader is doubtless aware, which will in a few years approximate to the Cremonese, if they escape the misfortune of falling into the hands of such gentry as I have before described!

Jerome Amati, of Cremona, by whom the oldest violins were made,* used the most beautiful maple with a very full figure, and, as far as I have been able to ascertain, constructed most of the backs of a single piece. The figure of the wood runs from the left to the right side, somewhat slanting downwards. The form of his violins is large, and the curves from one corner to another are most pleasing to the eye. The corners resting on the sides are very obtuse, and therefore

---

* That is, so far as the author's knowledge of the Cremonese instruments went (see the commencement of this chapter); but the head of the Amati family was *Andrew*, who was born about 1520, and died about 1580. See p. 63.—*Tr.*

c

do not extend far beyond them at the back, which produces a very handsome appearance. The edges of the back are very thick and beautifully rounded. The purfling, as in all the Italian instruments, is rather broad, and accords with the general structure. The model is not so flat as that of Straduarius, but somewhat higher. It rises so gently from the purfling (which is here placed rather farther inwards than in other violins), that, viewing the horizontal surface of the edge and the middle of the back, no one would think the highest part required an inch thickness of wood to work out this model, which seems so perfectly flat to the eye. The sides are also made of beautiful, full-figured maple, and do not run quite perpendicular from the back to the belly, but are so placed as to form an angle of a hundred degrees with the back, which gives the instrument a very elegant appearance. The corners of the semi-circular side-pieces are very obtuse, and those of the upper and lower side-pieces are slightly turned outwards. The sides, on the interior part, are furnished, both above and below, with thin strips of pine-wood, about a quarter of an inch broad, which are placed close against the back and also against the belly. The four corners of the semi-circular bendings are strengthened with little blocks of pine, an inch and a quarter broad, which fill up the corners in such a manner, that the inside of the violin resembles the form of an Italian guitar. At the upper end, where the neck is fixed, there is also a little block of pine, which rises gently from the sides, and is three-quarters of an inch thick in the middle. A similar block is placed at the lower end, into which the button for the tail-piece is inserted.

The belly, which has the same gentle rise as the back, is made of excellent pine-wood ; and, although the grain is not very fine, the fibres are perfectly equidistant, both in the middle and near the edges. The *f*-holes are beautifully shaped and stand rather near each other, so that the space between the upper little turns is only the breadth of the bridge ; they are particularly narrow at the upper and lower turns, and by no means wide in the middle. The edges and purfling are like those of the back.

The neck is made of the same beautifully-figured wood as the back and sides, and the cheeks of the peg-box are very strong and full. The scroll, which is admirably rounded, is very broad from the central point on one side to that on the other, and is indisputably the most beautiful form which has been adopted for violins ; indeed, of all the Italian violins which have come under my notice, those of Jerome Amati are the handsomest in shape and the most carefully made. They are covered with amber varnish mixed with a light reddish-brown colour *(kirschbraunen Lasurfarbe)*, which has greatly peeled off the majority of them. There are some which have a mahogany colour mixed with the varnish.

These are the oldest Cremona violins, as they were made during the years 1614—1620, and are now therefore (in 1817) two hundred years old. From their firm and good construction, however, they may retain their excellence half a century longer.

The above maker was followed by Anthony Amati, who was perhaps his son,* but of whose violins I have seen only a few ; so that probably most of them exist in Italy, France, and England. They are not very differently made from his

---

* This error of the Author has been duly corrected in the 1828 edition of his work, where Anthony Amati is properly named as the *brother* of Jerome.—*Tr.*

father's,* except that he was not so particular as Jerome in selecting beautifully-figured maple; but in quality of tone they are nothing inferior, if they have not been spoiled in repairing, like some which have come into my hands, the wood of which had been shamefully scraped away. As an instance of this, I may mention one which the Duke Ernest Augustus purchased for 200 ducats, the back and belly of which I was obliged to patch and strengthen on the inside with old wood, in order to restore the instrument to its true proportions; for it had been so damaged, that, considering its tone, it was not worth more than 5 dollars. As already stated, I have seen but few genuine instruments of Anthony Amati; and this has led me to infer that only few of them have been brought into Germany. There are, however, the more of Nicholas Amati, of Cremona, who flourished during the same period as Anthony Straduarius.

The violins of Nicholas Amati are particularly remarkable, as being of a rather smaller size, and having a peculiar model. They run rather flat from the purfling inwards, and then rise, more suddenly than those of either Jerome or Anthony, to an inch above the level of the side pieces, and form, in the highest part, a sharp ridge. This constitutes their chief characteristic. For the rest, his violins are not made with the extreme care as those of Jerome; the purfling is not let in so neatly, and the corners turn farther outwards: but the edges are very beautifully rounded, and the *f*-holes are well-shaped and stand rather near each other, as in all the Italian instruments. The interior of those which have escaped injury proves that he constructed on strict mathematical principles. An unspoiled violin of his make is

---

* His *brother's.—Tr.*

excellent, and almost preferable to a Straduarius, as the belly on the side of the fourth string does not bend in like [many of] the latter. The wood used for the belly is not of a very fine grain in any of them; but the back, neck, and sides are formed of beautifully-figured maple. All those which have passed through my hands have been covered with a reddish-yellow amber varnish: I have never met with one of a brown colour.*

The violins of Straduarius are distinguished for their very flat construction. The back and belly are not raised more than half an inch; consequently these instruments have the flattest model of all the Cremonese. Those which are un-injured possess a very beautiful, deep, and full tone. They are the most esteemed by public performers; for every virtuoso on the violin either has one already, or spares no expense in obtaining one. The reason of this probably is, that a flat-modelled instrument may be very thick in the wood and yet maintain a free and energetic vibration; and, indeed, it is an acknowledged truth, that an instrument which is thick in the wood possesses a much finer tone than one which has been scooped out.

But there is no doubt that many of these instruments have been greatly damaged; for, as they are constructed very flat and thick in the wood, on acoustic principles, and have a weak and rather short bass-bar, it has happened with many of them that the belly, on the side of the G string, has sunk in a little; or, when they have been tuned too high, it has risen on the opposite side, under the E string. Really great artists regard this slight defect as the natural consequence

---

* In the 1828 edition, Otto says: "They are mostly covered with a reddish-yellow amber varnish; I have only seen *one* brown."—*Tr.*

of age, and in no respect detrimental to the tone ; but amateurs, desirous of making improvements where none at all
are required, have had their violins taken to pieces on account
of the above-mentioned circumstance, and by the insertion
of long and heavy bass-bars checked the accurately calculated
vibration.* Yet, even in this case, if no wood has been
scraped away, this injury may be rectified by a maker possessed of the requisite knowledge ; but if any of the wood
has been taken out, the evil cannot then be corrected without
impairing the tone.

It has already been remarked that the model of the Straduarius violins is very flat : indeed, I have hitherto met with

---

* It is certain that the bass-bars were as accurately proportioned,
by the great makers Straduarius and Guarnerius, as all the other
parts of their instruments ; but the excessive rise in the musical
pitch which has taken place since the commencement of the
eighteenth century, and especially since Otto first published his
book, appears to leave us only the alternative either of suffering the
ultimate destruction of valuable violins, or of giving them somewhat
stronger bass-bars, so as to resist, in an efficient manner, the greatly
increased tension of the strings.

The celebrated Tartini found by experiment, in 1734, that the
strain of the four strings over the belly of a violin was equal to a
weight of 63 pounds, and the strings were then thinner and the
bridge less elevated than at present ; so that the angle formed by
the strings was considerably less than it is now. Five-and-twenty
years ago, the first string required a weight equal to 22 pounds,
in order to bring it up to pitch ; the second string required rather
more than 20 pounds, and the other two a little less. The total strain
was then about 80 pounds ; the pitch having risen a semitone since
1734, the strings being also thicker, and the angle formed by them
upon the bridge being more acute. The pitch having again risen
nearly a semitone since 1830, it would now doubtless be found by
experiment that the strain of the four strings on a violin is equal to
90 pounds or upwards. Hence the necessity of preserving the
masterpieces of the great violin makers from a strain which they
were never constructed to bear ; and hence, also, another argument
in favour of a reduction of the musical pitch. See M. Fétis's *Rapport*

none but what are higher. Their shape is very fine, but not so obtuse in the corners as those of Jerome Amati. The corners and edges are beautifully finished ; and the purfling is still broader than in the instruments of the last-named maker, and not inlaid very near the edge. The *f*-holes are finely cut and lie rather near together, as is the case in all genuine Italian instruments. The back, neck, and sides are made of very beautifully-figured maple,* and the instruments are covered with a dark brown amber varnish. Some of them have a yellow-brown varnish; but dark brown is the more usual colour. There are some which in shape closely approximate to the violins of Jerome Amati, and are also constructed rather higher than those before-mentioned. These have a mahogany-coloured amber varnish.†

---

sur les Instruments de Musique dans l'Exposition universelle de Paris, en 1855, p. 34. The strain or tension of the strings here commented on, while chiefly affecting the violin in a longitudinal direction, also exercises a vertical pressure on the belly of the instrument, where the bridge stands ; which is more or less according to the height of the bridge and the angle formed by the strings upon it. In 1840, Savart found this pressure to be equal to about 24 pounds. The Abbé Sibire, in 1806 (see *La Chélonomie*), estimated the tension of the strings at 64 or 65 pounds, thus indicating at that time but a very small rise in the pitch since the date of Tartini's experiment. Zamminer, in his very interesting work, *Die Musik und die musikalischen Instrumente* (Giessen, 1855), puts the tension at about 54 pounds ; but this may be a typographical error, unless, indeed, his investigations were made with thinner strings than those of Tartini and Sibire, which seems improbable. — *Tr.*

* In some of his violoncellos, in a tenor, and in viols of various kinds, he used poplar for the back, but this was contrary to his usual habit. — *Tr.*

† We are informed by Gallay, that M. Chanot, of Paris, (a brother of the naval officer mentioned at p. 74), once had under his hands a very curious specimen of Stradivari's workmanship, namely, a guitar-shaped violin, with a flat belly. (See *Les Luthiers Italiennes aux 17e et 18e Siècles*, Paris, 1869, p. 166). — *Tr.*

The violins of Joseph Guarnerius are very beautifully made. They are extremely similar in form and model to those of Nicholas Amati, as well as in the cutting of the *f*-holes, and have the same deep yellow amber varnish.

These, as well as the violins of Ruggerio and Albani,* differ so little from each other, that it is extremely difficult to give an exact description of them.

The violins of Jacob Steiner, of Apsam, differ from the Cremonese both in general appearance and in tone. They have a higher model, and their proportions of thickness are calculated quite differently.† Perhaps the most accurate comparison which can be drawn between the two, is, that the tone of a Cremonese violin resembles that of a clarinet, whilst the tone of a Steiner is similar to that of a flute.‡ The belly is modelled higher than the back; and the height of the belly where the bridge stands is equally maintained for half the length of the instrument to the lower or broad part [under the tail-piece], where it then diminishes down to the end edge. The breadth of this raised part is about the same as that of the bridge itself, and then it falls off towards the edges. The model is precisely similar towards the neck, and on the broad part [beneath the finger-board]. The edges are very strong and round, and the purfling, which is

---

* These are probably the makers intended by the Author, though their names are spelt *Rutgeri* and *Alwany* by him.—*Tr.*

† In the 1828 edition, Otto observes that Steiner made his instruments of three sizes—a large size, a medium, and a small.—*Tr.*

‡ Gretschel speaks of the Steiner violins as generally possessing a thin and penetrating tone, but that some exceptions to this exist (see p. 99 of the 2nd edit. of Wettengel's *Lehrbuch der Geigen und Bogenmacherkunst*, Weimar, 1869). Abele says they more nearly approach the sharp, piquant tone of the later German instruments. —*Tr.*

narrower than in the Cremonese (in which it is very broad), lies rather nearer the edges than in those instruments. The *f*-holes, which are rather shorter than in the Cremonese instruments, are beautifully formed, and their upper and lower turns are perfectly circular. The neck is particularly handsome, and the scroll as round and smooth as if it had been turned : some are finished with lions' heads, which are admirably carved. The sides and back are made of the finest figured maple, and the instruments are covered with amber varnish of a reddish-yellow colour. In some, the peg-box is dark brown and the belly deep yellow. These are their chief characteristics. Labels are rarely found inside ; but when these do occur in genuine instruments, they are always written ; printed ones being only met with in the Tyrolese imitations. In the Cremonese instruments, however, they are all printed.

The Tyrolese imitations of the Cremonese and Steiner violins may be especially recognised by the perfectly fine-grained larch-wood used in them, which differs considerably from the Italian, which is not so fine. Moreover, the depth of the sides in the Tyrolese instruments is rather less, the edges are not so strong and perfect, and the purfling is narrower and nearer the edges, which are not so finely rounded, but more of an angular form. The *f*-holes are pretty well imitated, and also the shape of the instruments, but the model is entirely false ; for those which bear the name of Jacob Steiner are very flat, and, on the contrary, those which have Cremonese labels are often high-modelled. The sides, back, and neck of most of the Tyrolese instruments are not made of figured, but of perfectly plain maple. The scroll is cut very small, compared with that of the Italians, and the difference in the proportion of all parts, between the genuine instruments and the imitations, is as three-fourths to one.

One of the most striking characteristics, however, is this : all the Tyrolese violins are covered with a weak spirit varnish of a greyish yellow cast, which, in order to give it an appearance of age, is laid on very thin, and soon wears off ; whilst the strong oil varnish on the old Italian instruments, however hard it may be rubbed, will remain firm and durable. This should be particularly observed by those who have not an opportunity of. instituting a comparison between several violins. If they are only able to distinguish amber varnish from spirit varnish, no Tyrolese violin can possibly be palmed upon them for an Italian one ; and it is with these Tyrolese instruments that people are most frequently deceived.

I will here briefly enumerate the German makers who have imitated the form of the Cremonese instruments, but under their own names. *Bachmann* of Berlin ; *George Schonger* of Erfurt ; *Jauch* of Dresden ; *Hassert* of Eisenach ; *Ernst*, Concert-director, of Gotha ; *Artmann* of Wegmar, near Gotha ; *Binternagel* of Gotha ; *Fritzsche* of Leipzig ; *Hunger* of Leipsic ; *Ulric Eberle* of Prague ; *Charles Helmer* of Prague ; and *Schmidt* of Cassel.*

---

* Particulars of some of these makers, not having been given in the previous chapter, are here inserted from the 1828 edition :—

"*Fritzsche*, of Leipzig, a pupil of Hunger, deserves to be ranked among the best and most skilful of the modern makers. Such of his instruments as are in good hands must continue to improve, as they are constructed with care and according to established rules. He has also highly distinguished himself as a repairer."

"*Frank Anthony Ernst*, a Bohemian by birth, who took up his residence at Gotha in the year 1778, was esteemed not only as a celebrated violinist, but also as a maker of violins after the Italian model. In Prague, where he studied, he employed himself with violin making by way of amusement, and, on coming to Gotha

Statelmann, of Vienna, and *Withalm*, of Nuremberg, have
made the greatest number of instruments after Steiner's
model ; both, however, under their own names. They have
also used the same deep yellow-coloured amber varnish,
which gives a still closer resemblance to the patterns they were
imitating. Those made after the Cremonese form by Jauch,
Hassert, Bachmann, Straube, Hunger, Eberle, and Helmer,
are likewise covered with amber varnish, and hence they are
more exact copies of the originals than are the Tyrolese ;
except those of Egitia Klotz, which, too, are distinguished
as well by their amber varnish as in other respects.

The foregoing characteristics of the Cremonese and Steiner
violins are also applicable to tenors and violoncellos : but
these instruments are much more scarce than violins.* In

---

reverted to this employment, after having neglected it for many
years. Now, however, he pursued it with extreme ardour, even
taking lessons in mathematics, in order that he might be wanting in
no information which could contribute to the perfect construction of
instruments. Nor were these efforts fruitless ; for having, as a
member of the Chapel, much time at his disposal, he had leisure
enough to give all diligence to the pursuit ; and whoever has become
acquainted with his violins must certainly admit that they possess
considerable merit. Even the Chapel-master, Herr Spohr, I have
been assured, has performed a concerto on one of Ernst's violins.
From him I received instruction in violin-playing, and soon took
delight in the manufacture of the instrument. Hence, he was my
teacher in a two-fold capacity. After I left Gotha for Weimar, he
took an assistant, the joiner *Artmann*, of Wegmar, near Gotha, who
afterwards manufactured violins very similar in form and model to
those of Ernst, which are very flat. Subsequently, another joiner
worked with him, of the name of *Bindernagel*, who has also made
violins which, in their exterior, are similar to Ernst's. The instruments of both, however, clearly prove that they were deficient in
the requisite knowledge."—*Tr.*

* According to Rochlitz, the older tenors had five strings, the
fifth answering to the E-string of our violins. Hence it is that the
Germans still call E-strings *quints* (i.e. *fifths*), although violins are

my professional travels, I have had only six violoncellos to repair, and two Cremonese tenors, and one of Steiner's, which belonged to the late chapelmaster, Herr Stamitz. Of new violins after the Cremonese model, I have made but a few for the chapel at Weimar, and six, together with a tenor and a violoncello, for the Chapel Royal at Copenhagen. I was prevented making more, through the following circumstance : the late Duchess Amelia of Weimar having introduced the guitar into Weimar, in 1788, I was immediately obliged to make copies of this instrument for several of the nobility ; and these soon becoming known in Leipzig, Dresden, and Berlin, so great a demand arose for them, that, for the space of sixteen years, I had more orders than I could execute.

I must here take the opportunity to observe that, originally, the guitar had only five strings. The late Herr Naumann, chapelmaster at Dresden, ordered the first guitar with the sixth or low E-string, which I at once made for him. Since that time the instrument has always been made with six strings ; for which improvement its admirers have to thank Herr Naumann.

---

only mounted with four strings, it having always been the practice in Germany, as we are told by L. Spohr, "to reckon the strings from grave to acute, commencing with C, the lowest string of the violoncello and tenor." (See p. 114 of the translator's edition of Spohr's Violin School, published by Messrs Cocks and Co.) About the year 1840, Herr Hillmer invented a five-stringed instrument which he called *Violalin*—a sort of compound of the violin and tenor, from having the addition of the low C-string of the latter. It was intended as well for the performance of violin compositions, as for those written for the tenor (and even for the violoncello, only, in this case, an octave higher). But instead of being an *invention*, it appears rather, from what is stated above, to have been a return to early usage. Leipzig *Allgem. Mus. Zeitung* for 1840, p. 245.—*Tr.*

During the last ten years, a great number of instrument-makers, as well as joiners, have commenced making guitars; so that, since that time, I have entirely relinquished the business, and now turn over any orders which I receive to my sons, at Jena and Halle, who are much occupied in that way. The use of covered strings for the D and G is a small improvement of my own. In the guitar, as brought from Naples, a large violin third-string was used for the D, and only the A was covered.

As I now hope to be more serviceable to the musical world in the construction and repair of bow-instruments [than in the manufacture of guitars], I shall henceforth employ my time in that manner.

CHAPTER IV.

OF THE REPAIR, PRESERVATION, AND METHOD OF BRINGING
OUT THE TONE OF INSTRUMENTS.

I WILL now state the rules necessary to be observed in endeavouring to improve faulty instruments; which reminds me that Herr Schubert, in the 47th number of the Leipzig *Musical Gazette*, for 1808, promised to publish a work on this subject; but I know not whether it has yet appeared.

The manner of taking off the belly is sufficiently known to all practical instrument makers. After the instrument has been taken to pieces, the back and belly must be measured with the double callipers, to ascertain whether both have corresponding proportions of thickness, and whether the breast is the thickest part. The middle of the back, too, of an equal breadth with the bridge, must be at least as thick as the belly. If this is found correct, and the cheeks are but a little thinner, and if the back and belly then diminish in thickness down to the edges, until they are only half the strength of the breast where they meet the sides and the upper and lower end blocks, the construction is mathematically true in the most important respect. But should any defect exist in the finishing of the instrument, which renders the tone coarse, or difficult of production, the fault lies in the bass-bar, which, from being too long, obstructs the vibration of the belly.*

---

* Wettengel and others say the bass-bar should be half the length of the belly, and equally thick throughout.—*Tr.*

The same difficulty in bringing out the tone arises if the bass-bar is placed too far inwards, instead of being more under the foot of the bridge; as it does not then receive the concussion direct from the bridge, but first from the wood adjoining, which cannot act so powerfully upon it. Sometimes, notwithstanding the seeming regularity of all the parts, the entire structure is too weak. Every different model, whether higher or flatter, requires different proportions; and it is in this respect that faults are often observable, as makers in general pay no attention to such difference.* But the Italian makers and Jacob Steiner thoroughly understood this matter; on which account their instruments, although massively and strongly made, still possess an extremely powerful tone, which arises from their accurate vibration. Instruments which have been finished off too weak, and in which the thickness of the back and belly is not in due proportion with the model, cannot be brought into a good state.

The bass-bar must be placed under the left foot of the bridge, with its upper end a quarter of an inch· nearer the middle joint [of the belly] than the opposite end which turns towards the cheeks, so as immediately to throw into vibration the fibres of the wood in the belly for the breadth of half an inch. This is the position of it in all good instruments. A violin constructed on the Cremonese model, and having the same thickness of wood as those instruments, will admit of being tuned up to pitch without sinking in, even in the absence of the bass-bar and sound-post: consequently these pieces are not inserted for the purpose of strengthening

---

* According to Abele (*Die Violine*, p. 96), even Statelmann and Withalm (so highly commended by Otto for their copies of Steiner, are not wholly free from the faults here alluded to. — *Tr.*

the instrument, but for promoting the vibration. It is much to be wished that some intelligent mathematician would closely investigate the origin and propagation of this vibration, which, to the best of my knowledge, has not yet been fully explained.*

It is of the utmost importance that the bass-bar be not too long ; for, otherwise, it checks the vibration, and renders the tone of the G-string remarkably weak, as compared with the rest, all of which are deteriorated, though not in so great a degree. But the chief defect occasioned by too long a bass-bar, is the want of resonance in the tone.

On many instruments, the F and F sharp on the D-string are quite dull and throbbing (pochend). This arises from the cheeks being worked out, according to a false theory, to half the thickness of the breast ; which is also frequently done after the whole has been finished. If the instrument be a valuable one, the best way to correct this fault would be to veneer it carefully with old wood of the proper kind ; but, in the case of a violin of less worth, a new belly would be the surest remedy.

If the wood has been scraped out of the breast, it is discovered by the defective vibration of the A-string, on which the C and C sharp have the same dull tone as before observed of the F and F sharp on the D-string. This, also, can only be rectified by restoring the due thickness of the wood.

----

* Some extremely interesting experiments on the violin have been made by Felix Savart. See *L'Institut*, 1ere Section for 1840, pp. 55, 69, 91, 122 ; or a German translation, *Ueber den Bau der Geige*, Leipzig, 1844 : also No. III of the Appendix. In chap. III of P. Davidson's treatise, *The Violin*, is likewise given what that writer designates a "*rough translation*" of Savart's lectures ; a statement much more accurate than some others he has made, to the detriment of his book which, in other respects, is not devoid of merit.--*Tr.*

Tho irregular vibrations are most clearly distinguishable in those notes which have no relation with the open strings.

The veneering such violins [with old wood] demands considerable skill, and in particular some knowledge of chemistry, in order to prepare a glue which may not be affected by the dampness of the atmosphere,* otherwise they will vary in tone as often as the weather changes.

I must now point out a fault which occurs in the interior of some irregularly constructed violins, which is, that the parts of the belly resting on the end blocks are often thicker than the breast. This construction is particularly detrimental, as it checks the vibration of the belly.

If an instrument has been injured by oil or any kind of grease getting inside, it must be taken to pieces and thoroughly cleaned, which can be done by chemical means.

I now proceed to notice the exterior of the violin. The neck is simply glued to the body—not fastened with either a nail or a screw, as in that case it could not be taken off without removing the belly. If the neck is in the right position, the surface of the finger-board must be parallel with it : for, if the finger-board is too thick next to the body of the instrument, the difficulty of playing will be increased, particularly on the shift. The finger-board is best when made of solid ebony ; for those which are veneered, and require to be leveled when they are worn down, do not last so long. A diligent player would, perhaps, find this leveling necessary

---

* A few drops of creasote in a pot of glue will, it is said, prevent this. A waterproof glue may also be prepared thus :—Immerse glue in cold water, until it has become perfectly soft, though still retaining its original form ; after which dissolve it in common raw linseed oil, aided by a gentle heat, until it becomes entirely taken up by the oil, after which it may be applied in the same way as common glue.—*Tr.*

every year. The rounding of the finger-board must conform exactly to that of the bridge : if it is too flat, the A and D strings will be too far from it ; in which case the bow is liable to touch the adjoining strings in performing passages of high notes ; and, if too round, then the E and G strings will be found too far from it ; which fault cannot be corrected by making the bridge rounder, as that would impede rapidity in playing. As regards the length of the finger-board, it should extend over the body as far as the upper corners of the semi-circular parts. The nut should stand as high above the finger-board as the thickness of a small pen knife, and have the strings let into it in such a manner, that the E string may be about as far from the finger-board as the thickness of a playing-card, and the other strings each proportionately a little farther from it ;* for the E string, having the greatest tension, consequently yields the shortest vibrations ; but the others [being slacker] may more easily strike against the finger-board.† From the termination of the neck, the under part of the finger-board must be hollowed out and worked gradually thinner down to the end. This does not injure it, as the fixing and leveling only extend to the end of the neck.

The tail-piece must likewise be made of ebony, and it is most advisable to have the holes and slits for securing the strings rather large ; but the distance of these holes must be

* Welcker von Gontershausen says the E string should be at the distance of two-hundredths of an inch, and the G-string of three-hundredths of an inch, from the finger-board. See p. 235 of his work before mentioned.—*Tr.*

† To afford greater space for the vibration of the G string, Spohr approves of the finger-board being hollowed out under it. See his Violin School, Part I., Sec. 2. Bernhard Romberg adopted the same form of finger-board for his violoncello under the C string; from whom, indeed, Spohr copied it.—*Tr.*

so adjusted, that the strings, in approaching the bridge, may be separated but little farther from each other ; otherwise, in tuning, they will be liable to draw the bridge forwards. The tail-piece should be two inches distant from the bridge, and it will be best secured to the button by a loop of E string, doubled and twisted.*

---

* The late celebrated L. Spohr invented a very peculiar tail-piece, by means of which the portions of the strings lying between it and the bridge could be so regulated as to produce certain intervals ; which might tend, perhaps, to modify little inequalities of tone in some instruments, or prove advantageous in other respects. The figures 5 to 10 will serve to give the reader a clear idea of this contrivance ; *Figs.* 5, 9, and 10 being drawn half the size, and the other three the full size of the tail-piece.

Fig. 5, consisting of a fore-part A and a hind-part B, is formed of a single piece of wood. The fore-part is perfectly flat at the top, but is worked out underneath, to the extent and in the manner shown in the section of the tail-piece, *Fig.* 9, and in the view of the front end of it, *Fig.* 10. This fore-part has four long openings (as at a, a, a, a, in the figure) placed at a suitable distance from each other, and made to receive the like number of little pegs, formed as in *Fig.* 7. The hind-part B of *Fig.* 5, which is semi-circular, stands a little lower than the fore-part A, and has its upper edge rounded off, as shown in *Fig.* 9. It is chiefly remarkable for four small slits, b, b, b, b (extending from the outside towards the centre), made to receive the knots of the strings, and for a little nut, c, formed of bone or brass, which is let into the middle of the semi-circular part B. There are also two small holes, d, d, through which the gut string is passed which connects the tail-piece with the button. Four other small holes pass obliquely from the upper to the under side of the tail-piece, as shown by the dotted lines, d, *Fig.* 9.

Figs. 7 and 8 are front and side views of the little pegs which are placed in the openings, a, a, a, a, of *Fig.* 5, and press on the strings beneath the fore-part of the tail-piece, as shown in *Fig.* 9. By moving them to and fro in their respective openings, those portions of the strings between them and the bridge are lengthened or shortened, and thus the different intervals are obtained. These pegs consist of two parts, as in *Fig.* 6, where a represents the knob, or cap, and b the pin which is firmly glued into a hole in the middle of it, after having been first passed through one of the openings, a,

Tho bridge is one of the most important pieces, and must be specially adapted to the instrument.* The best wood for it is the spotted maple, which must neither be too soft nor too hard. The grain of the wood should run in the direction of the breadth, and the top of the bridge should be only half as thick as the feet. The height must be accurately adjusted to the instrument; and in this respect it may be seen whether the maker possessed a scientific or merely a practical knowledge of his business; for the position of the bridge will be determined accordingly.

When the bridge is too high and too thick, it makes the tone dull, and difficult to be produced; and, when too low, the tone is shrill and piercing, and deprived of all power and fulness. If, after the height of the bridge has been adjusted, the finger-board should sink down a little, it must be raised by inserting a thin slip of wood underneath; or, if it should

---

Fig. 5, from the under side; the little furrow, *c*, at the bottom of the peg, is intended to receive the string.

From the section *Fig.* 9 the mode of attaching the strings may be seen. After tying a knot in the string, *a*, it is drawn into one of the slits, *b;* then carried over the nut, *c*, and passed through a hole, *d*, running obliquely from the upper to the under side of the tail-piece. It then passes into the furrow of the little peg, *e*, and over the bridge in the usual way.

Fig. 10 gives a front-end view of the tail-piece, with the four pegs fitted into their respective openings.

This ingenious invention has been but little used.—*Tr.*

* Besides forming a support for the strings, it serves to communicate the vibration from them to the body of the instrument; as may be proved by substituting for it a bent wire in the form of a slur ⌒, just long enough for the ends to rest on the edges of the violin, when the tone will be found to be considerably weakened. The application, too, of the mute, as is well known, also causes a remarkable subduing of the tone, by so tightly clipping the bridge as to partly check its vibration, and thus in some degree obstruct the communication above mentioned.—*Tr.*

fall considerably, the neck must be set back ; for the bridge must never be lowered, as that would impair the tone of the instrument. A good violin, in which the wood has not been scraped away, requires a somewhat higher bridge, as the instrument possesses greater strength of vibration. It is true that such a bridge renders all defects more perceptible, and generally the pressure of the strings is greater when the bridge is higher. Those instruments which are damaged and faulty, may be improved in some degree by a lower bridge; but in that case the tone certainly loses in power.*

The sound-post must not be too long, otherwise it will raise up the belly; nor must it be so short as to fall down when the bridge is taken off. The ends of the sound-post should fit against the back and belly with the greatest exactness; for on this the excellence of the tone considerably

---

* In the 1828 edition of his work, published at Jena, our author says that the suitability of the bridge depends more on its *weight* (consequent on its thickness) than on its *height;* for the latter regulates itself—at least, in part—by the position of the finger-board. He then describes the way in which he himself proceeds to ascertain the exact weight of bridge which any instrument requires, namely, by making six little pieces of wood into the shape of one-third part of a violin mute, and of the respective weights of 2, 4, 6, 8, 10, and 12 grains. These he tries successively on any bridge which he finds unsuitable, by placing them between the D and A strings, until the weight thus added to the bridge renders the tone of the instrument satisfactory. He then weighs the bridge and the little piece of wood together, and selects a new bridge of a weight precisely corresponding to the result, and which shall exactly balance the old one and the mute-shaped little block.

Mackintosh, in accordance with his theory, says :—"It is necessary that the timber of the bridge should have pores proportionate to those of the violin ; and to prevent this being left to chance, it is necessary to examine the wood of the bridge, and not put it on the violin unless it be of a quality suitable to that of which the violin itself is composed."—*Tr.*

depends. I have myself remedied many glaring defects of an instrument by means of a correct sound-post. In good instruments, the proper place for the sound-post is half an inch behind the right foot of the bridge ; but, in faulty ones, it may be placed rather nearer, in order to give greater fulness, and to improve the tone.*

The holes for the pegs should not be made too conical. The pegs themselves, the best of which are made of box-wood or ebony, must be fitted to the holes with a file. When they have worn smooth and will not hold, they should by no means be rubbed with rosin, chalk being much better for tightening them.†

The foregoing rules are also mostly applicable to tenors

---

* This statement of the author is supported by a remark of Welcker von Gontershausen, who, in his work published in 1855, p. 216, says that, in undamaged violins, the position of the sound-post is from 46 to 50 hundredth parts of an inch behind the right foot of the bridge. For some important remarks on the bridge and sound-post, the reader is recommended to consult Spohr's Violin School, Part I., Sec. 2.

A few years ago, hollow *glass* sound-posts were tried, and the results announced by M. Petizeau to the Academy of Sciences in Paris. "By this device," it is said, "very ordinary violins may acquire properties of sound only to be met with in instruments of the first order." In the Leipzig *Allgem. Mus. Zeitung* for 1811, p. 75, a German instrument maker and musician, John Anthony Hänsel, declares that numerous experiments and close comparisons have convinced him that "a broad, thin, and splinter-like sound-post is far preferable to the ordinary round form," although extremely difficult to set up, and requiring the greatest accuracy to ensure success.—*Tr.*

† Several mechanical pegs have been invented for the purpose of more perfectly resisting the tension of the strings, but they have not met with much favour from violinists ; perhaps on account of their expense (or, in some cases, their complexity), as a new set of wooden pegs can be soon fitted, when really necessary, at a very trifling cost. The simplest mechanical contrivance of the above nature, known to the editor, consists of a round-headed screw, which, being passed

and violoncellos, these being constructed and put together in the same way as violins. Tenors are often made out of the so called *Viole d'Amore;* but these instruments, from their construction, are peculiar for a soft and weak tone. Tenors which are made out of *Viole di Gamba* have a nasal tone, like a violoncello, and are therefore, at the most, only useful for quartetts.*

Should any alteration or repair be required when no experienced workman is at hand, the professor or amateur will at least have the satisfaction of knowing that, by scrupulously attending to the previous remarks, his instrument cannot be spoiled.

It is much to be regretted that all violin-makers are not likewise good players, and able properly to try their instruments, instead of being obliged to appeal to musicians for their opinion of their workmanship: for how different are the tastes of musical men, and by what prejudices are they biassed! One considers an instrument particularly good when it has been worked out very thin, and feels light in the

---

into the small end of the peg, presses a little plate of metal firmly against the outside of the peg-box; the peg itself being first cut just below the level of the outside of the box before the screw is inserted. —*Tr.*

* The *Viola d'Amore* was somewhat larger than a tenor, and originally mounted with twelve or fourteen strings, the half of which were of metal, and passed under the bridge and finger-board to the pegs. These were so placed merely to augment the tone by their sympathetic sound, being tuned in unison with the gut and covered strings, which rested on the bridge, and were played by the bow. Subsequently these metal strings were discarded, and, in the first quarter of the last century, Mattheson states that the instrument had only five strings, of which the four lower were covered.

The *Viola di Gamba* was nearly as large as a violoncello. It was mounted with six, and sometimes even with seven strings, and had a peculiarly nasal tone.—*Tr.*

haud; whilst this is really the greatest fault which it can possess. Another believes that an instrument is improved in tone by first breaking it to pieces and then joining it together again :* but this, too, is false; for glue is only a means for uniting pieces of wood, and cannot possibly augment the vibration. It may be, that if an instrument of faulty construction is repaired by an intelligent maker, its defects are corrected; in which case it is doubtless better than it was before : for a good instrument, if not too greatly damaged, may certainly be so far restored by the hand of a skilful workman as to discover no sensible loss of tone ; but assuredly no better tone can be produced by breaking it to pieces and then glueing it together again.

Other ridiculous experiments are made by blockheads, who torture their instruments by changing the bridge and sound-post until they will scarcely sound at all. Then they go to an instrument-maker, who, profiting by their simpleness, pretends that their instrument is too weak in the wood, and proceeds to lay on pieces where none are at all necessary : or he tells them that the bass-bar is too weak and short. It is then changed, and money earned. All this, however, only satisfies until the expenses are forgotten, when the experiments with the bridge and sound-post are again renewed, until at last the instrument is either exchanged or thrown aside as worn out or useless. The same fate would befall the concert-violins of Rode, Kreutzer, Spohr, or Möhser, if they had the misfortune to come into the hands of such gentry : but these are taken better care of, and their possessors, who know their value, prize them like their very eye-sight.

---

* This ridiculous idea was conceived by Maupertuis. See his paper, "Sur la Forme des Instruments de Musique," in the Mémoires de l'Acad. Roy. des Sciences, 1724, pp. 215—226.—Tr.

Persons of the above description spoil instruments even worse than a careless repairer, and seriously injure both themselves and their musical friends. About half a year ago [1817], I received two Tyrolese violins which had been in such a musical laboratory, which convinced me that these gentlemen were emulating the alchymist, who desired to convert his lead into gold, but obtained only ashes for his pains: and so it happened with their instruments.

Other very injurious experiments tried on violins have come under my notice, such as covering the belly with a mixture of glue and powdered glass : but this, instead of answering the object had in view, only tended to make the instrument worse. This injury, however, may be rectified. Another and irremediable damage has been done to violins by a late pianoforte-maker at Halle; who, conceiving the idea that they were too old, and that the wood had lost all its capability of producing a good tone, sought to restore it by dissolving rosin in pine-oil and soaking the instruments therein, which utterly ruined them. It is well for violins that this art died with Herr Weickert; at least, I have heard of no one following his example.

To describe other equally ridiculous experiments with varnish, white of egg, and so on, in order to close the pores of the wood—putting cross-beams on the back and belly— placing the sound-post on a strong cross-beam, &c. would be foreign to my purpose, which is simply to caution the public against the pretended improvements of such men, who are destitute of sound knowledge in respect to what is good or bad for instruments.* It were better to endure patiently

---

* Some of the more recent *inventions* and *improvements* of this stamp—or vagaries, as Otto, perhaps, would call them—are collected together in a note at the end of this treatise, pp. 50, *et seq.—Tr.*

a slight fault in a good instrument, than to expose it to a greater injury.

I will now briefly state what should be done for the preservation of an instrument. It is absolutely requisite that a good old violin should be kept in a wooden case, lined with woollen cloth or flannel ; as the too great heat in summer, and the sudden changes of cold and heat in the winter, are prejudicial to it. Too great a heat renders the wood brittle and the tone difficult to be brought out, besides drying up the strings, so that no delicate sound can be drawn from them. In winter, the too great warmth of a room produces the same results. When an instrument is removed in the winter from one house to another, without a case, it condenses moisture, on being brought out of the cold into a warm room, which causes dust to fasten on it, both inside and out, and forms a crust, which can only be got off with Dutch rush. Much greater damage is done to the instrument in summer, when left out of its case, as the flies crawl in at the f-holes, and in a few years so dirt the inside of the back and belly, that the wood feels like shagreen.

The instrument should be kept particularly clean, and the rosin-dust carefully wiped off with a linen cloth. The inside, too, should be cleaned every half-year with a handful of barley, made rather warm, and poured in at the f-holes. Then, by properly shaking the instrument, the dust will adhere to the barley and come out with it through the f-holes.

In order to preserve the strings a length of time in good and sonorous condition, it is necessary to keep a small piece of taffeta, moistened with almond-oil, in the bladder containing the spare strings, and, each time after playing, to rub the strings with it, from the bridge to the nut, before putting the instrument away in the case ; and when again wanted for use, the oil should be wiped off with a fine linen cloth, particularly at the place where the bow is applied. The advantages resulting from this plan are—first, that the strings, thereby receiving nourishment, will not become dry, but always retain their smoothness of tone ; and, secondly, they will not imbibe the moisture which exudes from the fingers and renders the strings dirty and false, so that they produce a grating or whistling kind of sound when the rosin is freely used ; all which will be obviated by the method here proposed.

This treatment of the violin was adopted by the concert-director, Ernst, under whom I studied music ; and on my recommending it to the professors and amateurs with whom I have done business, it has met with their unanimous approval. It is especially beneficial to the G-string, the gut of which dries up during the heat of summer, whatever stretching it may have received before being covered, and the wire then becomes loose. However, by the means here named, this is prevented ; for the string absorbs a little of the oil, between the coils of the wire, so that it does not get quite dry.

The best method of preserving the spare strings is to moisten them with almond-oil, and then wrap them up in a piece of calf's or pig's bladder, and enclose them in a tin box.

The best strings which I have ever seen are those from Milan, which are sold under the name of Roman strings, and may now be had at almost every music shop.* I will here

---

* The Neapolitan strings are now in high repute ; and those made by Savaresse, of Paris, are also greatly commended. See Gretschel's edition of Wettengel's *Lehrbuch der Geigen und Bogenmacherkunst* (Weimar, 1869), p. 211.—*Tr.*

mention the characteristics of the best strings ; for at Neu-kirch in Voigtland, in Bohemia, and in the Tyrol, some are manufactured which are falsely sold for Italian. The Milanese strings look very clear and transparent, like glass. The third string should be quite as clear as the first. They must by no means feel smooth, for they are not polished up like those of other manufactories. Further, if a good string be taken between the fingers and bent together, it will return to its former position like a watch-spring. Every string should look like a strip of glass on the finger-board; as those which are dull and opaque are good for nothing. Another characteristic of the Milanese strings is each being tied twice with red silk ; which, however, the Neukirch string-makers have also imitated. Their elasticity is, however, the surest characteristic : for all other strings which I have tried are comparatively weak and feeble.*

The quality of the rosin is a matter to which the player must direct special attention ; hence an intimate acquaintance with it is by no means superfluous. The brown rosin of commerce is unfit for a good violinist, as it hangs thick on the bow and strings, and occasions a rough or scratching tone. This caused musicians, about forty years ago, to attempt at refining it, which they thought to accomplish by boiling it in vinegar ; but, being unacquainted with chemistry, their experiments were fruitless. Boiling the rosin in vinegar

---

* In the present day the Acribelle or silk strings are much approved by some violinists, as they are said to be very durable, almost ten-sionless, and impervious to moisture—a great consideration with those who have a warm hand. Gretschel informs us (in the second edition of Wettengel's *Lehrbuch*, before mentioned) that, at a recent exhibition in Paris, violin strings were shown which were made of human hair ; but these, while yielding a good sound, were not found to be durable.—*Tr.*

certainly made it harder ; but, as it became incorporated with the vinegar, it acquired an opaque yellow colour, and, owing to the moisture it contained, clung to the bow and strings even worse than before. Had they known how to make it clear and transparent again, it would have been improved ; but in that state it was not so. My instructor procured rosin from Prague, which looked like fine transparent amber, and possessed all the good qualities that could be desired in it. In the first place, it took hold [of the strings] very well, without scratching ; secondly, it did not lie thick upon the strings, but dispersed in dust ; and, thirdly, it kept the hair of the bow very white and beautiful.

Having a knowledge of chemistry, I spent both time and money, thirty years ago, in endeavouring to imitate this rosin. However, I soon attained my object, and have since been rewarded for my labour, by the great quantity I have sent to the musical establishment of Dittmar and Gerstenberg, in Russia, without reckoning what I supplied to the chapels with which I did business.

As some of my readers may, perhaps, be inclined to try experiments of this kind, I would observe that the basis of the common rosin is too coarse, and that, in order to obtain it perfectly good, only Venetian turpentine must be used.*

---

* After a perusal of these remarks, and a due regard to the amount of chemical knowledge implied in them, the reader may feel somewhat astonished at the summary manner in which the subject is treated by Maugin (*Manuel du Luthier,* p. 138). "Behold the secret which is nothing :—Melt some common rosin in a new, glazed, earthen pot, over a moderate coal fire ; and, as it dissolves, filter it through a rather coarse new linen cloth into a second pot of the same kind as the other, taking care to keep it near the fire ; afterwards pour the rosin into little rolls of paper, or make it up into tablets for use."

Otto himself, in the 1828 edition of his work, says :—"Put a

As good instruments are constantly becoming more rare, it is necessary to think of some compensation. For some time past, as before remarked, I have been hindered from making violins, through the manufacture of guitars; but now having four sons who follow this business, I am at length enabled to resume my usual occupation. I shall therefore be happy, with the assistance of my sons, to undertake the construction of violins after the Cremonese form, and with a strict observance of their model, a point which is seldom attended to. These instruments, as well as tenors and violoncellos, shall be made, according to the principles of mathematics and acoustics, of sonorous Italian wood, and covered with amber varnish, like [that which] the old makers used; as the wood will not absorb the moisture of aquafortis and spirit; besides, it possesses greater durability than spirit varnish, and is therefore in all respects preferable for violins, &c.

My instruments may be had on order, either quite new, or perfected by a machine for bringing out the tone, of

---

pound of Venetian turpentine into a new earthen pot, add some water to it, and then let it boil for two or three hours over a slow fire. As the turpentine rises to the surface, cold water must be kept ready to pour in whenever it threatens to run over; and, even if no such tendency appears, water must be added from time to time, otherwise the turpentine will be boiled too much and become burnt. The sign that it has boiled sufficiently is, when a drop, which has been allowed to cool on a plate, rubs clear between the fingers, without sticking. When it is so far ready, pour it into cold water, and work it well through the hands, so as to express the water which it has taken up in boiling. When quite cold, break it into little pieces, and, in the summer, let the sun extract the remaining moisture, until it becomes perfectly transparent. In the winter, it must be put into a porcelain vessel in the oven; not so hot as to fry it, but only so warm that the water contained in it may be gently evaporated. In this manner beautiful and clear rosin is obtained."—Tr.

which a further account will appear in the *Musikalische Zeitung.* *

It may be received as an established truth, that an instrument acquires a beautiful and mellow tone, not by age, but by constant use.†

I have some ordinary-made violins which had been used by a village musician, for twenty years in playing dances, and, being in a damaged condition, I purchased them at a trifling price. Finding, on examination, that they were strong in the wood throughout, and had good pine-wood bellies, I tried what could be made of them by a proper

---

* If the author here alludes to the Leipzig *Musikalische Zeitung,* no account of his machine has appeared in that work.—*Tr.*

† Mackintosh also states that *age* is not one of the essentials of a good violin ; "although," says he, "it is a very generally received opinion that a violin, intrinsically bad, may become possessed of a first-rate tone when it can boast of an existence of at least half a century ; but such is not the fact. And, in proof of the assertion, I may here observe that there is a far greater number of *old violins bad than good.*" And, again, he says—"*Age* is not necessary to constitute a good violin, since those changes in the wood, so essential to tone, which hitherto age alone has been acknowledged to bring about, can be effected previous to the construction of the instrument." He likewise supports Otto's views in reference to the effect of use, by remarking that, after the observance of all the rules of construction, violins "have to be ultimately perfected by the influence of proper playing." The fallacy respecting the superlative merit of mere age has likewise been noticed by M. Fétis in his "*Rapport sur les Instruments de Musique dans l' Exposition universelle de Paris, en* 1855," p. 31. Abele and Welcker von Gontershausen also insist on the absolute necessity of constant playing, in order to perfect the tone of a well-made violin. The former author has been already quoted on this point, in note †, p. 13. The latter remarks that age is only beneficial under certain conditions ; namely, when the instrument is diligently and skilfully played on, when strings of unvarying sizes are preserved, and when these are always kept at a uniformly high pitch. But, he adds, an unplayed violin does not improve.—*Tr.*

finishing and arrangement *(Aptirung)*, and obtained a violin which, although every judge knew it to be a trade instrument, was not inferior in tone to an Italian one ; and for which the concert-director at Fulda gave me forty dollars. This led me to imagine that constant vibration shakes the resinous particles out of the wood, thereby rendering it more porous and better adapted for producing a good tone, than it otherwise is. I therefore made the experiment with the continual sounding of two notes forming an interval of a fifth, to ascertain whether it would improve them ; and in the course of an hour I found they were much less rough and metallic in tone, than any others on the violin.

Having now discovered that, by sounding two notes at once with a powerful stroke of the bow, greater vibration was produced in the instrument, I further tried it by fourths throughout the scale. In this instance, also, every note equally experienced the desired improvement, and the keys of A flat major and C major became as good as those of D or G major.* I forbear to state the reason of this, from a

---

* The Author still advocates the method here referred to for bringing out the tone, in the 1828 edition of his book ; but instead of describing the machine mentioned at p. 47, he says : "Whoever attempts to bring out the tone of a new violin in this way, must first provide himself with a rather strong bow of pear-tree wood, the head and nut of which must be two inches high from the stick, and the hair be screwed rather tighter than a violoncello bow. He must also have a piece of silk cord, two or three ells long and as thick as a violoncello D string. After stringing the violin in a suitable manner and tuning it to concert pitch, he must stick a strip of white paper, four inches long and one broad, on the finger-board, beginning close against the nut, and draw lines on it corresponding very exactly to the places of the notes B flat, B, C, C sharp, D, and D sharp of the A string. The violin must always be kept strictly to the same pitch, which must be tested by a tuning fork."

"The instrument is now to be taken between the knees, and the

sense of duty to my children, and shall merely notice the progressive changes in the tone.

When a new violin is first strung, the tone is clear, harmonious, and easily produced; but, after exercising it for eight days, in the manner described above, it becomes harsh, and offensive to the ear, so that the instrument seems as if it would never be fit to be heard again; (in this second stage, perhaps the greatest number of instruments are spoiled, from the want of patience in the possessor, by scraping out the wood, changing the bass-bar, and other fancies; those, also, which are too weak in the wood, now become bad, and do not improve afterwards—they never reach the third stage :)

---

bow applied, with both hands, on the D and G strings, which are to be sounded together for a quarter of an hour; and then proceed in like manner with the other open strings. In this way all the other fifths are to be brought out; in order to do which, the silk cord must be used as an artificial nut, by passing it between the strings and the finger-board, and first binding it precisely over the stroke answering to B flat. The fifths A flat and E flat, E flat and B flat, B flat and F, being thus prepared, each of them must be sounded for a quarter of an hour, as before."

"The cord is then to be bound a semitone higher, and the sounding proceeded with until the fifths C sharp and G sharp, G sharp and D sharp, D sharp and A sharp are arrived at, when all the semitones occurring in the different major and minor keys will have been brought out."

"By this method, a new violin can be so improved, in two or three months' time, as to produce a fine, sweet, and powerful tone—fit for concert use; and it will then be worth twice as much as it was before."

In order to ensure the most complete success in this matter, it is obviously requisite to exercise the utmost care in selecting the strings, and in applying them to the instrument: for, as nearly all strings are somewhat thinner at one end than at the other, unless the thinner ends of the two adjacent strings are mounted on the instrument in the same direction, perfectly true fifths are unobtainable in all parallel positions on the finger-board. To assist the performer in the choice of perfectly equal strings throughout their length, an instrument called a *Phonoscope* was made some years ago, by König, of Paris, and which is said to have been very successful.—*Tr.*

E

but, by persevering in the practice of two notes together. the third stage is gradually attained; at which the instrument, like wax, receives every impression, and the tone, having recovered its power and fulness, again becomes clear and beautiful. This, however, requires three months to effect: hence, a violin so exercised cannot be afforded under thirty dollars, nor a violoncello under fifty.

I have now only to state that I reside at Halle, where, in conjunction with my sons, I undertake to bring out the tone of instruments in the way above-mentioned. Should any of my kind patrons and friends require to write to me, I beg that their letters may be addressed to Jacob Augustus Otto, at Halle, instrument-maker to the University: and, in conclusion, I desire to express the hope that the present little work may not be wholly devoid of interest to the musical world.*

---

* As an instance of the strange freaks that have been played with violins (and against which the Author has so strongly declaimed), it has been deemed desirable to give some account in this place of sundry novel vagaries; with the object of supplying the reader with information on the subject of violin manufacture down to the present time, rather than for any benefit which the interesting art has derived from these novelties !

Of freaks relating to the bass-bar, the following have come under notice :—

1. M. Rambaux, of Paris, exhibited at the *Exposition Universelle*, in 1855, a violin with *two bars:* one fixed in the usual position under the belly ; the other glued to the back, and having the sound-post placed upon it. The instrument, although originally indifferent, was by this means so much improved that, according to the testimony of several distinguished performers, it yielded a free, equal, and powerful tone. It also possessed a remarkable degree of sonority on the fourth string ; a feature supposed to be produced by the coincidence of the energetic vibrations of the two bars, rendered normal by the influence of the sound-post. For instruments constructed according to the admirable principles of the great Italian makers, the addition of a second bar was deemed altogether unnecessary ; while at the same time it was clearly proved that those of a less perfect character were sensibly ameliorated thereby.—See M.

Fétis's "*Rapport sur les Instruments de Musique dans l'Exposition universelle de Paris, en* 1855," p. 34.

2. In the French Exhibition of 1867, M. Miremont showed some violins with a second bar (for which he took out a patent), extending from the top and bottom blocks inside. This was found to be the reminiscence of a system proposed some fifteen years previously by an American maker, named below. M. Miremont, it appears, did not declare his secret to the jury, who failed to perceive the results in his instruments !

3. Wm. B. Tilton's (American) *Improvement*, introduced into this country about the year 1852, consisted of a bar placed as Miremont's above mentioned, the upper and under surfaces of the end blocks to which it was fastened being sloped inwards, to prevent contact with the back and belly of the violin, so as to leave these parts more free to vibrate.

4. Dr. Stone's and Mr. Meeson's elliptical tension bars. This invention was brought before the members of the Musical Association at their first meeting (Nov., 1874), and is thus described in one of the notices which appeared soon afterwards :—" Four strips of white deal, curved to an elliptical figure, pass parallel, from end to end, on the inside of the belly. Thus they intercept the *f*-shaped sound-holes, and remove a well-known cause of weakness and a break in the vibrating body," &c. It is further said—"Dr. Stone asserted that, by the adoption of this process, a common instrument can be made nearly equal in tone to an old Italian fiddle !"

Against this opinion must be set that of M. Gallay, who, in commenting on changes made in the barring of violins up to the time of the publication of his work, in 1869, says :—" All attempts at improvement have yielded nothing but deception." An anecdote, also, in reference to *Tilton's Patent Improvement*, may likewise here find a place. Charles Maucotel, who formerly carried on the business of a violin-maker in London, having heard of Tilton's Improvement, obtained one of the violins fitted with the new bar, which was examined by some connoisseurs, and created the greatest admiration. They even went so far, as the Editor is informed, to rank the instrument equal in tone to that of some old Italian violins with which it was compared. In their exuberance of delight at so wonderful an achievement, they promised, on leaving, to bring others in a day or two to see the novel invention. Maucotel, however, who was an adept in his art, believing that the violin would sound as well without the precious bar as with it, opened the instrument after the gentlemen had left, took out the bar, and again adjusted the violin apparently as before. On the return of the gentlemen, with their friends, the "Patent Improvement" violin was tried and re-tried, with the same admirable result as on their former visit; when Maucotel—satisfied as to the correctness of his own views—declared to them the bar had since been removed, and forthwith he submitted it to their inspection. A retreat was, of course, soon inevitable; and after that he heard no more of Tilton's Improvement ! It is only necessary to add that the identical bar which Maucotel thus experimented upon can be seen at Mr. George Chanot's, in Wardour Street.

Of novel forms of violins, two of which were shown in the Exhibition held at Munich, in 1854, the so-called *Trumpet-violin* of Ferd. Hell (which seems to have been patented in this country, in the same year, by W. E. Newton) is so thoroughly ridiculous, that nothing more need be said of it than to state the tube of a trumpet was coiled up inside, with the bell end opening (as far as the depth of the body of the violin permitted) towards the button of the tailpiece, and the smaller end of the tube connected with the mouthpiece passed down the neck, and out at the scroll. Abele says that neither the tone of the trumpet nor that of the violin was bad.

The other novelty of this kind in the same Exhibition, consisted of a string quartett, made by A. Engleder, of Munich, and possessed the following peculiarity of form. The upper half of each instrument was contracted, and passed almost perpendicularly into the curves, wholly omitting the upper corners ; whilst the lower half, also omitting the corners, was expanded nearly in a proportionate degree to the contraction at the other end, so that the outline resembled that of a pear. As might be expected, nothing very favourable could be reported of these queer-shaped instruments.

In the London International Exhibition of 1862, Mr. Hulskamp, of New York, but a native of Westphalia, showed a violin which was so constructed as to admit of a regulated tension of the back and belly. This was effected by a simple mechanism within the instrument, which was acted on by a key, and thus (according to the Jurors' Report), the tension of the tables could be readily put in harmony with the strings ; so doing away with the necessity of giving a bulging form to the back and belly, which being made quite flat, instruments of the finest quality could, it was stated, be constructed with certainty at a far less cost than usual. Instead of the ordinary *f*-holes, this instrument had a small circular opening in the belly, between the bridge and the end of the finger-board. One foot of the bridge rested on the belly, and the other on a post, which passed through the belly (but without touching it) and stood on a rib fastened to the inside of the back. The names of Messrs. Joachim, Laub, and Becker are mentioned as having expressed favourable opinions on this new invention ; which, however, seems to have had its day, like other novelties.

APPENDIX.

No. I.

METHOD OF TRACING A BEAUTIFUL MODEL FOR A VIOLIN, BY
MEANS OF A GRADUATED PERPENDICULAR LINE.*

AFTER having prepared the wood for the back and belly
in the manner stated in the first chapter of this work, and in
the form described in *Fig.* 1, draw a perpendicular line down
the middle of the flat side of the piece intended for the back,
of the exact length required for the body of the instrument,
and divide it into 72 equal parts, as shown in *Fig.* 4. This
must be done with the greatest accuracy, for on it depends
the correctness of the whole.

---

* From Wettengel's *Lehrbuch der Anfertigung und Reparatur
aller Gattungen von italienischen und deutschen Geigen* (Ilmenau,
1828), which has been preferred to a somewhat similar method by
Bagatella, on account of its greater completeness, &c. The original
tract of Bagatella, published at Padua, in 1786, being difficult to
obtain, those who wish to see his method may consult the German
translation of J. O. H. Schaum, *Ueber den Bau der Violinen,
Bratschen, Violoncells und Violons* (Leipzig), or the works of
Wettengel, Gretschel, Welcker von Gontershausen, Zamminer, or
Abele, mentioned in the present treatise. The method put forth as
Bagatella's by P. Davidson (see *The Violin,* pp. 115 *et seq.*) is
spurious, although given as genuine by Maugin, in his *Manuel du
Luthier* (Paris, 1834).—*Tr.*

Then intersect this perpendicular by twenty horizontal lines, at the points named below:

Line		at the point
Line	1—A	8
——	2—B	14
——	3—C	16
——	4—D	20
——	5—E	$21\frac{1}{4}$
——	6—F	22
——	7—G	23
——	8—H	27
——	9—I	28
——	10—K	31
——	11—L	33
——	12—M	34
——	13—N	37
——	14—O	39
——	15—P	40
——	16—Q	$44\frac{1}{4}$
——	17—R	48
——	18—S	55
——	19—T	56
——	20—V	65

This being done, open the compasses to an extent of 9 parts ot the perpendicular, and describe the two arcs a, a, from the point b. Then place the compasses on the point 24, and, opening them to b, draw the curve a, b, a.

Next, set off two parts c, on each side of the perpendicular, on the horizontal line C. Place the compasses on the points c, and, opening them to a, draw the curves d, from a to the horizontal line A.

Now set off one part e, on each side of the perpendicular, on the line B. Place the compasses on these points, and, opening them to the line A, where the curve *d* ends, draw the curves *f*, from the line A to that of D. This completes the draught of the upper portion of the instrument.

For the middle or narrow portion, proceed thus :—On the horizontal line L, set off $11\frac{1}{2}$ parts, from the perpendicular to *g*; and then 11 other parts, from *g* to *h*; from which latter point draw the curve *i*, from the line L to that of P.

Next, set off $23\frac{3}{4}$ parts on the line K, from the perpendicular to *k*; open the compasses to the point where the curve *i* intersects the line M, and draw the curve *l*, from the line M to that of H. The little angle formed by the curves *l* and *i*, between the lines L and M, must be worked off so as to bring the sides into the proper shape.

The lower portion is obtained as follows :—Open the compasses 11 parts and describe the two arcs *v, v*, from the point *rr*. Then place the compasses on the point 35, and, opening them to *rr*, draw the curve, *v, w, v*.

Next, set off six parts *x*, on each side of the perpendicular, on the line S. Place the compasses on the point *x*, and, opening them to *v*, draw the curves *y*, from *v* to the line V.

Now set off four parts *z* on each side of the perpendicular, on the line T. Place the compasses on these points, and, opening them to the line V, where the curve *y* ends, draw the curves *aa*, from the line V to that of R.

For the upper corners, set off $24\frac{1}{2}$ parts on the line G, from the perpendicular to *o*, and, placing the compasses on this point, open them to the line D, where the curve *f* ends, and draw the curve *p*, from the line D to that of F.

Then, on the line I, set off $14\frac{3}{4}$ parts, from the perpendicular to *m*. Place the compasses on this point, and, opening them to the line H, where the curve *l* ends, draw the curve *n*, from the line H to *s*.

Now, on the line E, set off 22 parts, from the perpendicular to *q*. Place the compasses on this point, and, opening them to where the curve *p* meets the line F, draw the curve *r*, from the last-named line to *s*.

Again, place the compasses on the point 20, and opening them 16⅓ parts, mark off the length of the corners, *s, s*.

For the lower corners, set off 24 parts on the line Q, from the perpendicular to *bb*, and, placing the compasses on this point, open them to the line R, where the curve *aa* ends, and draw the curve *cc*, from the line R to *dd*.

Then, on the line N, set off 16½ parts, from the perpendicular to *t*. Place the compasses on this point, and, opening them to where the curve *i* meets the line P, draw the curve *u*, from the last-named line to *dd*.

Lastly, place the compasses on the point 49, and, opening them 19¾ parts, mark off the length of the corners, *dd, dd*.

This completes the entire model, and the belly can now be marked from this pattern.

To obtain the proper height or rise for the back and belly, take a thin piece of hard wood, of about two fingers' breadth, and a little longer than the violin, and mark it in the middle, at the point A (see *Fig.* 2), which must be three-parts of the foregoing scale distant from the edge, shown here by the dotted line. Then, placing a large pair of compasses on the point A, open them 216 parts—or three times the length of the body of the instrument—and with this radius describe the arc B A B, which, by being sawn out, will serve as a guide for the height or rise required.

Of the different Degrees of thickness of the Back and Belly.

In regard to the back, take the point 42 for a centre and describe two circles, the first with a radius of 4½ parts, and the second with a radius of 12 parts, as shown in *Fig.* 4. Then carefully work out the wood comprised within the inner circle, until the back is reduced precisely to one part in thickness. From the first circle to the edge of the second, the thickness must very gradually diminish to two-thirds of a part; and from thence to the places where the back joins the sides, it must again as gradually diminish to one half of a part.*

For the belly, take the point 40 as a centre, and describe two circles, the first with a radius of 4 parts, and the second with a radius of $8\frac{1}{2}$ parts (see *Fig.* 3). Work out the wood comprised within the inner circle, until the belly is there left two-thirds of a part thick. Then, from the first circle to the edge of the second, the thickness must gradually diminish to one-half of a part; and from thence to the places where the belly rests on the sides, it must again diminish to one-third of a part.†

Of the f-holes or Sound-holes.

These should extend from the point $32\frac{1}{2}$ to the point $46\frac{1}{4}$, as in *Fig.* 3. The centre of their upper round holes should fall opposite the point 34, and that of their lower, opposite $44\frac{1}{2}$.

The radius of the upper round holes must be two-thirds of a part, and that of the lower, seven-eighths of a part. The

---

* The small semi-circular piece, described in *Fig.* 4 by a dotted line above the point *b*, forms part of the back, and is made of an equal thickness. It serves as a finish to that end of the neck which joins the body of the instrument, to which it is, therefore, shaped.

† Abele says that Steiner and Jerome Amati worked out the thickness of the wood, not in a circle, but in the form of an ellipse, whose longer axis was in the direction of the length of the violin. (See *Die Violine,* pp. 131, 132.)—*Tr.*

central points of these upper holes must be 10 parts distant from each other, and those of the lower holes, 25 parts distant.

The outer notches must fall opposite the point $39\frac{1}{8}$, and the inner, or bridge notches opposite the point 40, and at the distance of 8 parts from it. The f's, at the places wher. these notches occur, must be one part and one-third broad. The other particulars as to the shape and proportions can be gathered from *Fig. 3.*

Of the Bass-bar.

The bass-bar must be 36 parts in length, one part and one-fifth in breadth, and two parts thick in the centre, diminishing to two-thirds of a part at each end. Its place is exactly on the margin of the inner circle, parallel to the graduated line,* and at the distance of one-third of a part from the upper round of the left f-hole, with its centre opposite the point 40.

Of the Bridge and Sound-post.

The diameter of the sound-post and the length of each foot of the bridge must exactly coincide with the breadth of

---

* So say Wettengel, Maugin, and Bagatella ; but Otto (*vide ante,* p. 31) says its upper end must incline a quarter of an inch nearer the middle joint of the belly. Abele (*Die Violine,* p. 140) relates an anecdote of Stoss, of Vienna, from which it appears that he thought it a matter of indifference ; but such does not seem to have been the opinion of the Cremonese makers. The author of *Lutho-monographie* (that book full of errors !) maintains the bar should be set in the middle, exactly on the joint, on the ground of symmetry ; by which he supposes uniformity of tone will be obtained on all the strings ! This position of the bar was adopted by Savart in his trapezoid violin, and by Chanot in his guitar-shaped instrument (see pp. 73 and 74).—*Tr.*

the bass-bar. The distance between the inner points of the feet of the bridge must be just twice as great as that of the bass-bar from the graduated line. It must be set up in such a manner, that the half of its thickness may be on each side of an imaginary line passing from the inner notches of the *f*-holes through the point 40, and with the outer points of the feet at the same distance from each *f*.

The thickness of the upper corners of the bridge must be four-sevenths of a part, and that of the soles of the feet four-fifths of a part. Its extreme height, in relation to the length of the body of the instrument, must be as 16 to 193, for violins and tenors; and as 65 to 492, for violoncellos and double-basses.

The sound-post must be 11½ parts long, and placed, as shown in *Fig.* 3, in a line with the right foot of the bridge, and with its centre opposite the point 42.

Of the Sides, Side-linings, Blocks, and Neck.

The sides, which are placed at the distance of five-elevenths of a part from the edges of the back and belly, must be one-third of a part in thickness. Their breadth, for violins and tenors, must be 6¼ parts at the button, diminishing gradually to 6 parts at the neck; but, for violoncellos and double-basses, 12 parts at the button, diminishing gradually to 11¼ parts at the neck.

The side-linings should be one-half of a part thick, and about a part and a half broad.

The upper block must be 10 parts broad and 4 thick, and the lower block, 8 parts broad and 4 thick; their depth should conform to the width of the sides. The four corner blocks, too, must be 8 parts broad, and shaped as in *Fig.* 3, whereby the interior of the instrument acquires the form of a guitar.

The length of the neck must be 26 parts, measuring from the body of the instrument to the nut.

With the exceptions above stated, the present description applies equally to the tenor, violoncello, and double-bass.

No. II.

FURTHER NOTICE OF THE CREMONESE MAKERS AND SOME OTHERS.

The author having mentioned so few of the Cremonese makers in the 3rd chapter of this book, a brief notice of others, extracted from the highly interesting work of M. Fétis, on the celebrated Stradivarius,* will doubtless be acceptable to the reader.

But before giving particulars of the Cremonese, a reference must be made to the earlier school of Brescia, which included several makers of excellence, at the head of whom must be placed :—

Gaspar, Gaspard or *Gasparo di Salo,* so named from his having been born in the little town of Salo, on the lake Garda, in Lombardy. He worked at Brescia from 1560 to 1610, and was particularly renowned for his viols, bass-viols, and violoni, or double-bass viols. Some violins exist

---

* *Antoine Stradivari, luthier célébre : précédé de Recherches historiques et critiques sur l'origine et les transformations des instruments à archet,* Paris, 1856 ; a translation of which, by the editor, has been published by Messrs. Cocks and Co.

of his make, which are highly distinguished for their fine quality of tone.

Giovanni Paolo Magini, or *Maggini*, was born at Brescia, and worked there from about 1590 to 1640. He is particularly distinguished for his violins, which are of a large pattern and have similar dimensions and analogous workmanship to those of Gaspar di Salo, whose pupil he probably was.[†]

Pietro Santo Magini, another maker of Brescia, and probably of the same family as the preceding, worked in the seventeenth century. Although he made violins, he is chiefly celebrated for his double basses, which are renowned in Italy as the best instruments of this class.

Javietta Budiani and *Matteo Bente*, of the school of Brescia, flourished about 1580. They are both artists of merit, though inferior to Giov. P. Magini. The instruments of Bente are still sought for by those who form collections.

The founder of the great school of Cremona, and head of the celebrated Amati family, was :—

Andrew (Andreas) *Amati*, who descended from an ancient family of Cremona. The exact date of his birth is unknown, but it must have been during the first twenty years of the sixteenth century. He probably died about 1580.

Jerome (Hyeronimus) and *Anthony* (Antonius) *Amati* were the sons of Andrew. Anthony was born at Cremona, about 1550. He succeeded his father, and was for some time in partnership with his brother Jerome. The violins made by them during this period are highly esteemed. On

---

[*] *Antonio Mariani*, of Pesaro, a contemporary of Magini, made violins from 1570 to about 1620 ; but, as he worked at random and without determinate principles, his instruments are valueless, and are not even sought for as objects of curiosity.—*Fétis.*

the marriage of Jerome, the brothers separated. Anthony Amati probably died in 1635, as none of his instruments bear a later date. His brother Jerome died in 1638.*

Among the pupils of Jerome and Anthony Amati we must notice *Gioacchino* or *Giòfredo Cappa*, who flourished at Cremona in 1590. In 1640 he established himself at Piedmont, and there founded the school of Saluzzio, where the reigning prince then dwelt. He made a great number of instruments, and formed good pupils, among whom are *Acevo* and *Sapino*, whose productions, though not equal to those of the Amati family, are still esteemed. The best instruments of Cappa are his violoncellos.

Nicholas (Nicholaus) *Amati*, the son of Jerome, and the most celebrated of all the makers of this name, was born Sep. 3rd, 1596, and died Aug. 12th, 1684, at the age of 88 years, according to the registers of the cathedral of Cremona.

Jerome Amati, the son of the preceding Nicholas, worked

---

* These particulars, as before observed, are drawn from the work of M. Fétis. However, a well-known amateur, the late Rev. R. F. Elwin, in a letter addressed to the editor in 1848, mentions two violins which had fallen under his notice. The first (then belonging to Dr. Sommerville, of Stafford) bore the following label: "*Antonius et Hyeronimus F.* (ratres) *Amati, Cremonenses, et Andreæ Fil* (ii). *F.* 1648." The second, formerly the property of Wilhelm Cramer, father of the late François Cramer, and, in 1848, in the possession of Mr. George Vyall, of Norwich, had a similar label, except that the date was 1691. Mr. Elwin likewise quotes two other instruments, and gives the names of their possessors, from which it would appear that both Anthony and Jerome had each a son named Nicholas. The labels stand thus : "*Nicholaus Amatus Cremonen: Hyeronimi filius, et Antonii Nepos. Fecit* 1679 ;" and "*Nicholaus Amatus, Antonii filius, ac Hyeronimi Nepos, in Cremona.* 1644." Again, he mentions another with a label precisely similar to the last, but dated 1665. All these instruments he believed to be genuine; but *query ?—Tr.*

with and succeeded his father.   He was born Feb. 26th, 1649, and was the last violin maker of the Amati family.

The pupils formed by Nicholas Amati, are: His son, Jerome, Andrew Guarnerius, Paolo Grancino (who settled at Milan, and worked from 1665 to 1690), and the illustrious *Antonio Stradivari* or *Stradivarius*, of Cremona.

The following makers are generally considered as belonging to the school of Amati, either because they worked under Jerome, the son of Nicholas, or because they were formed by the pupils of this school, and followed the traditions of it with more or less exactness.

	Flourished.
Joseph Guarnerius, son of Andrew, of Cremona..................................	from 1680 to 1710
Florinus Florentus, of Bologna....	from 1685 to 1715
Francis Rugger, or Ruggieri,* surnamed *il Per*, of Cremona.....................	from 1670 to 1720
Peter Guarnerius, brother of Joseph, and second son of Andrew	from 1690 to 1720
John Grancino, son of Paolo, of Milan...	from 1696 to 1720
John Baptist Grancino, brother of John, of Milan	from 1690 to 1700
Alexander Mezzadie, of Ferrara	from 1690 to 1720
Dominicelli, of Ferrara.................. ..	from 1695 to 1715
Vincent Rugger, of Cremona	from 1700 to 1730
John Baptist Rugger, of Brescia	from 1700 to 1725
Peter James Rugger, of Brescia	from 1700 to 1720
Gaetano Pasta, of Brescia..................	from 1710 to ......
Domenico Pasta, of Brescia	from 1710 to ......
Francis Grancino, son of John, and grandson of Paolo, of Milan	from 1710 to 1746

---

* This name is sometimes spelt *Ruggerio—Tr.*

Peter Guarnerius, son of Joseph, and

    grandson of Andrew, of Cremona... from 1725 to 1740

Santo Serafino, of Venice .... from 1780 to 1745

Anthony (Antonio) *Stradivari* or *Stradivarius** was born in 1644. His early violins were made like those of his master, Nicholas Amati, and signed with his name. In 1670 he first began to sign his instruments with his own name. During the following twenty years, to 1690, he only produced a few. The year 1690 was one of transition in his career, but still he preserved the traditions of the Amati school, and his violins of this period are commonly called *Stradivarius-Amatis.* His finest instruments were constructed from 1700 to 1725; during the subsequent five years, to 1780, the workmanship of them is not of so high an order; and in 1730, or even a little earlier, the impress of Stradivarius is almost entirely lost. The instruments were then evidently made by less able hands; many, however, were signed by him as having been made under his direction, "*sub disciplina Stradivarii.*" In others we recognize the hand of *Carlo Bergonzi*, and of the sons of Stradivarius—*Omobono* and *Francesco.*

After the death of Stradivarius, the instruments remaining unfinished in his workshop were completed by his sons. The greater number of them bear his name; and hence the uncertainty and confusion in regard to the productions of the last period.

Stradivarius made but few tenors, and all of a large form. He made a greater number of violoncellos, which are of two

---

* This is the correct Italian or Latin orthography, of which *Straduarius*, as used by the author of this work, is evidently a corruption.—*Tr.*

dimensions : one large, which were formerly called *basses*. the other smaller, and properly called *violoncellos*. These instruments are greatly superior to all others of this class.

The discovery of a violin, of the date of 1736, and in which Stradivarius has stated his age, proves that he finished the instrument when he was 92 years old! He had prepared his tomb in 1729 ; but, strange to say, neither the remains of himself nor those of his children, were deposited therein. He was buried Dec. 19th, 1737, and therefore probably died on the 17th or 18th of the same month. His family consisted of three sons and one daughter ; of whom, two of the former worked in their father's shop until his death.

At the head of the best pupils of Stradivarius must be placed *Joseph Guarnerius* and *Carlo Bergonzi*. The latter was the more exact imitator of his master, and made excellent instruments. *Francesco Stradivarius* also made good violins, which, from about 1725 to 1740, bear his name ; other productions, achieved in conjunction with his brother *Omobono*, bear the inscription " *Sotto la disciplina d'A. Stradivarius, Cremona.*"

Omobono Stradivarius occupied himself more particularly with the repair and fitting up of instruments, than with their manufacture. He died in the beginning of June, 1742, and was buried on the 9th. His brother Francis only survived him eleven months, as he was interred on the 13th of May, 1743. Both rest in the same tomb with their father.

The other immediate pupils of Stradivarius are :—*Michael Angelo Bergonzi*, of Cremona ; *Laurence Guadagnini*, of Cremona ; *Francis Gobetti*, of Venice ; *Alexander Galiano*,*

----

* This name is usually written *Gagliano*.—Tr.

f

of Naples. They are ranged in the following chronological order, according to their productions :—

1st. Franciscus Gobettus, Venetiis .... 1690 to 1720
2nd. Alexander Galianus, Neapoli .... 1695 to 1725
3rd. Lorenzo Guadagnini, Cremonæ............ 1695 to 1740
4th. Homobonus Stradivarius ⎱ sub disciplina ⎱ 1700 to
5th. Franciscus Stradivarius ⎰ A. Stradivarii ⎰ 1725
6th. Homobonus Stradivarius, Cremonæ ...... 1725 to 1740
7th. Franciscus Stradivarius, Cremonæ.........1725 to 1730*
8th. Carlo Bergonzi, Cremonæ .... 1720 to 1750
9th. Michael Angelo Bergonzi, Cremonæ ...... 1725 to 1750

Of the Italian violin makers of the third rank, some have been raised in the Amati school, and others have been formed by the immediate pupils of Ant. Stradivari. They may be ranged in the following chronological order :—

Pietro della Costa, of Trevisa..................... 1660 to 1680
Michael Angelo Garani, of Bologna .... 1685 to 1715
David Techler, of Rome......................... 1690 to 1735
Carlo Giuseppe Testore, of Milan .... 1690 to 1700
Carlo Antonio Testore, of Milan .... 1700 to 1730
Paolo Antonio Testore, of Milan .... 1710 to 1745
Nicolo Galiano, of Naples .... 1700 to 1740
Gennaro Galiano, of Naples .... 1710 to 1750
Spiritus Sursano, of Coni (Cuneo).............. 1714 to 1720
Tomaso Balestiere, of Mantua .... 1720 to 1750
Ferdinando Galiano, son of Nicolo, of Naples 1740 to 1780
Giovanni Battista Guadagnini, of Piacenza ... 1755 to 1785
Carlo Landolfi, of Milan .... 1750 to 1760
Alessandro Zanti, of Mantua 1770
Laurentius Sturionus (Storioni), of Cremona 1780 to 1795

---

* This seems to be a typographical error. It should evidently be 1740, from what is stated at p. 67.—*Tr.*

Some violin makers, born in foreign countries, have been formed in Italy in the school of Amati, or in that of Ant. Stradivari. At the head of these must be placed Jacob Stainer, the founder of the Tyrolese school, who worked during his youth at Cremona, under Nicholas Amati.* The genuine instruments of this maker have been classed into three epochs. To the first belong the violins dated from Cremona, all of which have written labels, signed with the hand of Stainer : these are of the greatest rarity. So much obscurity reigns over the second epoch of Stainer's career, that we can only say he lived and laboured at Absom (his native place) from 1650 to 1667. It is said that he was here assisted by his brother, Mark Stainer, who was a monk. According to tradition, Stainer retired to a Benedictine convent, after the death of his wife, and there ended his days. In this seclusion, he determined on closing his career by the manufacture of twelve violins of superior finish, which he sent to the twelve Electors of the empire. M. Fétis saw one of these instruments, in 1817, and speaks most highly both of its quality of tone and varnish.

Matthias Albani, who sprang from the school of Stainer, was born at Botzen or Bolzano, in the Italian Tyrol, and died at the same place in 1678. His son, also named *Matthias*, was born at Botzen in the middle of the seventeenth century. After learning his trade from his father, he worked in the Cremonese manufactories, and made many instruments which have been esteemed nearly equal to the Amati violins.

---

* P. Davidson (see *The Violin*, p. 141) says Stainer was first a pupil of Anthony and afterwards of Nicholas Amati. *Luthomonographie* (p. 58) denies this *in toto*, and says that he was a pupil of *Albani!* The reader can place what reliance he thinks proper on these statements. —*Tr*

There was another Albani, who worked in Sicily, during the first half of the seventeenth century. Nothing is known of his life, nor is his Christian name given in the violin quoted by Fétis.

Matthias Klotz, a Tyrolean maker, was the best pupil of Stainer. He worked from 1670 to 1696. Other instruments of later date, bearing the same name, are believed to have been made by his sons; who did not set their own names to the violins and tenors which they made until the death of their father. The names of his sons were *George*, *Sebastian*, and *Egitia*.

Among the foreigners to Italy who worked under Ant. Stradivari, we remark—

Medard, who made violins, first at Paris and afterwards at Nancy, from 1680 to 1720.

Ambrose Decombre, of Tournay, who, in returning to his country, worked from 1700 to 1735, and whose basses are much esteemed.

Francis Lupot, of Stutgard, who worked there from 1725 to 1750. He was the father of him of the same name who established himself in Paris in the second half of the eighteenth century.[*]

John Vuillaume, of Mirecourt, who made good instruments from 1700 to 1740.

We now come to mention the family of *Guarneri* or *Guarnerius*, which furnished several distinguished makers of violins. The head of the family was:—

Andrew Guarnerius, born at Cremona in the first part of

---

[*] And to whom the Abbé Sibire was indebted for the greater portion of his work, entitled *La Chélonomie, ou le parfait Luthier* Paris, 1806.—*Tr.*

the seventeenth century. He was one of the first pupils of Nicholas Amati, and worked from 1650 to about 1695. His instruments rank in commerce among those of the second class.

Joseph Guarnerius is generally considered the eldest son of Andrew, and is said to have been brought up under his father. He worked from 1690 to 1730. He did not follow Andrew's model ; but first imitated Stradivarius, and afterwards his cousin, who was named Joseph, like himself. His instruments are of good quality, and esteemed.

Peter Guarnerius, the second son of Andrew, worked from 1690 to 1725. His first productions are dated Cremona ; but later he settled at Mantua.

There was another *Peter Guarnerius*, the son of Joseph, and grandson of Andrew. He made violins and basses at Cremona from 1725 to 1740.

Joseph Anthony Guarnerius (called "*del Jesù*," on
†
account of the initials I. H. S. which occur on the labels of his instruments) was the nephew of Andrew, and the most renowned of all those bearing his name. He was born at Cremona, June 8th, 1683, became a pupil of Ant. Stradivarius, and worked at Cremona from 1725 to 1745. His early instruments are not much esteemed, but those which followed a few years later are highly prized, especially those which are of a large model, and which are considered equal in merit to those of his celebrated master.

In the latter part of his life, he produced instruments altogether inferior to those which have caused his name to be so highly regarded. This has been attributed to his idle and dissolute habits, and to his having been imprisoned during several years for some cause still unknown. While in confinement, it is stated that the daughter of the gaoler procured him wood and some wretched tools, and that she assisted him in his work. The girl also purchased varnish for him, sometimes from one maker and sometimes from another, and sold the instruments at a low price, in order to procure him some relief in his misery. If all this be true, it accounts for the great change in the merits of his instruments, compared with those which he had before made.

Some of the Italians have imitated this maker, particularly *Paul Anthony Testore*, of Milan ; *Charles Ferdinand Landolfi*, of Milan ; and *Laurence Storioni*, of Cremona. All their instruments, however, rank among those of the third class.*

No. III.

SOME ACCOUNT OF THE EXPERIMENTS MADE BY THE LATE FELIX SAVART.

i i ι ι̯ ¹

(Born, June, 30, 1791. Died, March, 1841.)

THE highly important character of the acoustical investigations of M. Savart, relative to the structure of bow-instruments, cannot fail to interest all those who desire to

* In M. Gallay's work, *Les Luthiers Italiennes aux* 17e *et* 18e *Siècles* (Paris, 1869), Carlo Bergonzi and Domenico Montagnana are mentioned as immediate pupils of Joseph Guarnerius. Carlo Bergonzi is, however, usually held to be a pupil of Stradivarius (see *ante*, p. 67). Montagnana, who worked at Cremona and Venice from 1700 to 1740, has left instruments of a very high order ; his basses, in particular, being excellent.—*Tr.*

become acquainted with the causes—so far as they have
yet been ascertained—which tend to render some violins
(and chiefly those of the renowned Italian makers) so greatly
superior to others. It must, however, be remembered that,
in all scientific researches, and specially in those of such
extreme delicacy as are connected with the phenomena of
sound, *absolute certainty* in the deductions drawn from
experiments is not, or at least ought not to be, professed :
for the wisest philosophers may, and often do, find it necessary to relinquish former opinions—though apparently well-
founded—and to adopt others which subsequent investigations prove to be more correct.

And so it was with M. Savart, whose early researches, in
1817, led him to conclude that the violin would be improved
by taking the form of a trapezoid ;* in pursuance of which
idea, he himself made an instrument, differing from the
ordinary shape of the violin in the following particulars† :—
1st, the back and belly were flat, and narrower at the end
which joined the neck, than at the other on which the chin
rested ; 2ndly, the bass-bar was set in the middle of the
belly, under the joint ; 3rdly, the sound-holes were cut
straight, in the direction of the grain ; 4thly, the sound-
post was placed very near one of the sound-holes ; 5thly,
the sides were made straight and deeper than usual, and, as
this interfered with the action of the bow, on the two outer
strings, 6thly, a higher bridge was adopted to meet the

---

* For drawings and a more copious description of this instrument,
together with much interesting matter connected with Savart's
experiments, see his *Mémoire sur la construction des instruments à
cordes et à archet*, Paris, 1819, mentioned on the following page.—*Tr.*

† See an article on the subject in the *Magazine of Science*, Vol. V.
pp. 277—8. London, 1844.—*Tr.*

difficulty. In 1819 Savart presented a memoir on the subject of his violin to the French Academy of Sciences, who appointed a commission to report upon it. The violin was tried and re-tried before the members of the Commission, by M. Lefebure, who also compared it with the fine instrument on which he was accustomed to perform ; and the result was, that the new violin was pronounced equal, if not superior, to the other.*

Notwithstanding this flattering commendation, M. Savart still continued his researches ; and, on minutely examining

---

* In 1817 and 1819, M. Chanot, a naval officer and musical amateur, also received the highest praise from the Royal Academy of Fine Arts, in Paris, on the trial of his newly-constructed violins before a commission of that body. These instruments differ from the ordinary form of violins in several respects ; and the considerations which led to some of the changes appear to have been almost, if not entirely, identical with those which occasioned the variations in Savart's trapezoid violin ; but, notwithstanding the enthusiasm which they at first created, M. Fétis assures us that no one would now give 10 francs for one of them, except as a mere curiosity. It seems that M. Chanot at first proposed to add frets to the finger-board ; but this, being justly disapproved of by the Academy, was afterwards abandoned.

The peculiarities of these instruments were, then, as follow :—

1. The corners, with the inner blocks, were rejected, and the violins assumed the outline of a guitar, having the sides similarly bent.

2. The edges, instead of projecting beyond the sides, were finished off square, with an inlaying of hard wood all round, like the edges of a guitar.

3. Instead of sound-holes of the ordinary form, the new violin had openings of about the same length as usual, parallel to the sides, and as near the bendings as possible. Their shape was consequently that of a segment of a circle.

4. The bass-bar was placed in the middle of the belly, just upon the joint.

5. A screw was placed in the end of the tail-piece, near the button, which, by pressing on the belly, lifted the tail-piece, so as to

the instruments of Stradivarius, Guarnerius, &c., new light burst upon him, and the pre-eminent skill of these renowned makers soon became manifest.

For a full detail of the valuable results which now followed his investigations, the reader is referred to the works named in the note at page 32, as space can here only be afforded for the principal features.

The use of different kinds of wood for the back and belly of violins appears to have been adopted on good grounds. For the belly, as is known, *deal* is employed ; for the back, *maple,* or sometimes beech ; the former, however, being used in all the best instruments. Deal is preferable to every other wood for the belly, on account of its feeble density, and

---

prevent the strings forming too great an angle in passing over the bridge, and so causing too great a pressure on the belly.

6. Beneath the sound-post, and passing out through the back of the violin, was a screw, by means of which the pressure of the sound-post against the belly could be augmented or diminished.

Subsequently, namely, in 1819, the following changes were also made :—

7. The tail-piece and button were discarded, and the strings attached to the belly of the violin, midway between the outer edge and the bridge. The belly was veneered with a strip of hard wood, both inside and outside ; then holes and slits were pierced quite through to receive the strings, which passed over a little nut (forming part of the upper veneer) on to the bridge.

8. The bar was shaped in the form of an arch. It passed under the left foot of the bridge, near the G string, and approached the middle at the extremities.

9. The sound-post was placed in front of the bridge, instead of behind, as usual.

See *Description des Machines, et procédées specifiés dans les Brevets d'Invention*, &c. Tome xv., pp. 161—179. Paris, 1828.

The criticism of M. Fétis on these instruments (some of which possess an excellent tone) is not quite borne out by facts, as Mr. George Chanot, of London, informs me he has sold two of them for £12 and £8 respectively.—*Tr.*

particularly for its elasticity. Its resistance to flexion is greater not only than that of any other wood, but also than that of many metallic bodies. It is equal to that of glass and even steel, with the additional merit of very great lightness; and sound is propagated in it with the same degree of rapidity as in the other substances above-named. This is proved by taking three rods of equal size, one of glass, another of steel, and a third of deal (cut in the direction of the fibres), and causing them to vibrate longitudinally or transversely, so as to make them produce the same mode of vibratory division; when it will be found that the sound rendered by all three is precisely the same.

In maple, the propagation of sound is much less rapid than in deal. In the latter it is from 15 to $16\frac{1}{2}$ times quicker than in air; while, in the former, it is only 10 or 12 times quicker, in the direction of the fibres. Hence it follows, that if we take two rods of precisely the same dimensions, one of deal and the other of maple, and put both into vibration, the sound of the deal rod will be decidedly more acute than that of the other.[*] Consequently, the pieces forming the belly and the back of the

---

[*] This fact, as declared by Savart, should be well remembered, as it tends to throw a light on the circumstance that M. Fétis, both in his *Rapport sur les instruments de Musique* (Exp. Univ. de Paris, 1855) and in his book on *Antonio Stradivari* (English Edit., p. 83), states, when the *back* and *belly* were severally put into vibration, the former was exactly one tone *lower* than the latter; while Savart himself is made to say, in the analysis of his lectures given in the French paper, *L'Institut* (No. 321, for Feb. 20, 1840, p. 70), precisely the reverse. Now, it is necessary to observe, that at least two errors of a gross description occur in the analysis above-named, which have been most faithfuly preserved in the German translation mentioned in the note at p. 32. This naturally creates a suspicion in regard to the disagreement between the statements of

violin being exactly of the same size, do not possess an identical intonation.

If the back and the belly were both made of deal, or the former of a thinner plate of maple than usual, in order to obtain the two pieces in unison, Savart's experiments showed him that the tone of a violin so formed would be feeble and mediocre. It then became necessary to ascertain in what relation of sound the back and belly should stand to each other, before they are united. For this purpose Savart closely examined and experimented upon several valuable instruments by Stradivarius and Guarnerius, and discovered that there should be the difference of a tone between them : for, if less than that, beats were occasioned; and, if more, the vibrations coalesced with difficulty into the unison.

In order to obtain the true sounds of the back and belly, these pieces were placed in a vice, between two bits of cork shaped like a cone, at a point where two nodal lines, one transversal and the other longitudinal, crossed each other. This was ascertained in the usual way, by sprinkling the

---

Fétis and Savart; while, with the German translation in their hands, it is not surprising that several modern German authors have given precisely the same account of the relative vibrations of the back and belly as that attributed to Savart. Hence the counter statement of Fétis has been deemed inaccurate ; but, *query ?* The late J. B. Vuillaume not only supplied Savart with violins to experiment upon, but also induced Fétis to put together the materials relating to Stradivari, which he (Vuillaume) had collected during his journeys into Italy ; and being an able man in his art, and an enthusiastic lover of the scientific researches into violin making conducted by his friend Savart, he could most easily have corrected Fétis, had he considered his statement erroneous. Other reasons could be adduced in favour of the statement made by M. Fétis ; but, to save further detail, the above must suffice.—*Tr.*

surface with very fine sand, and putting the pieces into vibration by a violin bow applied to the edges; and the same nodal system being produced in each, the relative difference of pitch was easily found by means of the bow.

Savart remarks that the fibres of the deal should be perfectly parallel to the axis of the violin, and the different parts very symmetrical. In order, also, to judge the better of the relative merits of different pieces of deal, he directs to take a rectangular rod of each, of exactly the same dimensions, and worked up in the direction of the fibres, to put them into vibration longitudinally, and to select that which gives the highest sound. Such a rod may then be kept, as a standard of comparison, for future use.

The intensity of the sounds rendered by a violin was found, by Savart, to depend on the mass of air which is contained within the instrument itself, and which must be in a certain relation with the other parts. When this either exceeds or falls short of a given quantity, a detrimental effect on the tone is produced, as some ingeniously conducted experiments fully proved.

The sound yielded by the mass of air in several violins of Stradivarius was always found to be equal to that having 512 vibrations in a second, and answering to the pitch of middle C when these instruments were made; but, in 1838, when Savart made his experiments, it agreed with the B natural below; and, from the constant rise in pitch which has since taken place, it is now nearly in unison with B flat. The same result, as to pitch, was obtained when the back and belly of these violins were put into combined vibration, the sound yielded being equal to that of the mass of air, or 512 vibrations in a second. This, indeed, was found to be a general law, no matter what was the form of the violin; the mass of air within the instrument, and the combined vibration of the back and belly, giving the same sound; and thus forming a system of which the various parts re-acted on each other.

The dimensions of the f-holes exercise an important influence on the mass of air contained within the instrument. Thus, if we stick a piece of paper over one of the f-holes, the sound of the mass of air is sensibly lowered : consequently, if these holes are made smaller than usual, the sound of the air becomes more grave ; while, if, on the contrary they are made larger, it is more acute. Hence it happened that the mass of air in the large-modelled violins of Magini, which Savart examined, and which might naturally have been expected to render a lower sound than the C of 512 vibrations, nevertheless produced one more acute, namely D, because the f-holes were made larger than those of Stradivarius.

From the foregoing particulars it will be seen that it is possible to make violins of any form, provided the conditions mentioned be carefully observed. Thus, the height of the sides must be so proportioned to the size and thickness of the back and belly, as to enclose a mass of air which shall render a sound equal to 512 vibrations in a second ; which, however, admits of modification (as in the violins of Magini above-named), by the size of the f-holes.* But all changes of form produce an effect on the quality of the tone ; and it

---

* Excellent violins may be made in another key, by constructing them like those of Stradivarius, and taking care to preserve the same proportional dimensions, so that their relation may be as the vibrations of C natural to the new key. For example, violins may be made, the dimensions of which are to those of Stradivarius, as 512 is to the number of vibrations of, it may be, C flat ; and then put the enclosed mass of air in C flat.

has been remarked that the more a maker differs from the excellent proportions of the ancient models, the worse his instruments become.

In regard to the sound-post, Savart says, it must not be supposed that it acts merely as a conductor of sound, serving only to propagate the motion ; because, if placed outside the violin, its action still remains the same. This he ascertained by a peculiar contrivance suited to the object he had in view. He further proved it by removing the sound-post, and placing a heavy weight on the belly of the violin, which then sounded just as if the post had remained in its usual place, until the weight employed exceeded a certain limit.

By several other interesting and very delicate experiments, Savart found that the chief function of the sound-post is to render normal the vibrations of the back and belly ; the transversal oscillations of which produce in the sound-post a longitudinal motion, which, re-acting on that of the back and belly, occasions in them a normal movement.*

Another and no less important function of the sound-post is, to preserve the right foot of the bridge, behind which it is always placed, in a state of almost complete immobility, in order that the left foot may (as in the instrument called the *Trumpet Marine*) communicate its movements to the bass-bar.

---

* In regard to the term *normal*, as used by Savart, it is necessary to make a few remarks in this place, as Mr. P. Davidson, in his book on *The Violin* (Glasgow, 1871), p. 70, says : "Bishop, the translator of Otto's work, was evidently not aware of Savart's meaning." The editor having failed to elicit from Mr. D. the proof of his assertion, the reader may safely place the statement in the same category with others in that book, such as "*do* ♯³ represents 4 feet, or middle C," p. 73 (middle C, as is well known, answering to the 2 feet measure !) ; "a reed pipe consists of a free reed in communication with a column of air above it," p. 77 (the *striking* reed

This bar has the effect of producing, throughout the length of the violin, the vibration which is communicated to it by the bridge. It vibrates in its entirety, without any division, and so does the belly of the instrument.

The bridge, which at first sight might be thought to be only a necessary support for the strings, exercises an immense influence, both in its form and in its supposed merely ornamental cuttings, on the quality of the tone of a violin. Various forms have been successively adopted for it, of which engravings may be seen in the work of M. Fétis on Antonio Stradivari, but that which is now generally followed has been proved to be the most satisfactory; and any alteration made in it tends materially to affect the sonority of a good instrument. Savart found that when he took a plain piece of wood, of the size of a bridge, and glued it on a violin, the instrument had scarcely any sound. It became better when legs were formed to it; and, when too lateral cuttings were made, the tone assumed some degree of value, which increased as the bridge was gradually brought into the usual form. A succession of other experiments all tended to prove, that any change made either in the kind of wood, or in the form of the bridge, was invariably attended with a detrimental effect upon the quality of the tone.

---

being that in general use, and the *free* species the rare exception, in organ pipes, at least in Great Britain), &c. ! !

Of the three kinds of vibration now recognized—the *longitudinal* (in flat surfaces, also called *tangential*), the *rotary* (or that in which the vibrating part moves alternately to the right and the left), and the *transversal*—the first two were discovered by Chladni (who died in 1826), while the third—the transversal—has been known to scientific writers for a period now amounting to centuries, and hence some French authors and others have termed it *normal*. Behold, then, the profundity on which Mr. D. has thought it requisite to comment! See Bindseil's *Akustik*, Potsdam, 1839, pp. 30, *et seq.*—*Tr.*

The same skill which presided over the construction of all
the parts of bow-instruments, particularly of the violin, has
established the form of the neck, and determined the nature
of the wood of which it is made. All has been nicely calculated, in order that the vibratory action of this part of the
instrument might be in relation with the movements of the
sonorous body, the sound-post, the bridge, and the strings.
Although unperceived, incessant flexions and returns take place
in the neck of a violin, under the action of the bow upon the
strings, and these movements re-act upon the whole structure
of the instrument. When the neck is made either of too
stiff, or of too soft wood, its vibrations remarkably change
the nature and character of the sounds produced.

All that has been here related is likewise applicable to the
other bow-instruments, brief particulars of which, drawn from
Savart, will now be given.

Tenors. The mass of air in a Tenor should render a sound
a fifth below that of the C of a violin, consequently the F of
341.33 vibrations in a second, answering very nearly to our

present E flat ; but, the instrument-makers being

unacquainted with these principles, it is found that the
greater number of Tenors give precisely the same sound as
the violin C, of 512 vibrations.*

---

* This circumstance caused the late J. B. Vuillaume, in 1855, to
introduce a new model for the tenor, which was very broad and
high, and somewhat more difficult to play. Four of these instruments, which possessed a fine and powerful tone, were tried in the
concerts held at the Brussels Conservatory, and produced an effect
equal to eight of the ordinary kind.—Another novelty of this sort
was the *Violon-Tenor* of M. Dubois, sen., the four strings of which
were tuned an octave below those of the violin. See Gretschel's
edition of Wettengel's *Lehrbuch*, 1869, p. 221.—*Tr.*

Violoncellos should be so constructed that the mass of air within them might yield a sound corresponding to the F of 170.66 vibrations in a second, agreeing very nearly with E flat ♮ of our present pitch. If their dimensions were in due proportion to those of violins, the back and belly should be 85 inches long, and 20 wide; while they are ordinarily but 26 or 27 long, and 15 or 16 wide. As a compensation for this, however, the sides are made deeper, being 4 inches instead of 8; and, in thus augmenting them, the makers have been able, without, perhaps, knowing why, to produce a satisfactory result; by causing the enclosed mass of air to render a sound very nearly a twelfth below that of the mass contained in a violin, as indeed the instruments require.

Double-basses. Up to the present time these instruments have not attained the same degree of perfection as others played with a bow. They are made of all sizes, and strung and tuned differently in different countries.* Some of the best instruments of this class, by Gaspard di Salo and Magini, are said to have been originally made for double-bass viols, with large necks, and mounted with six strings; but, in more recent times, they have been furnished with smaller necks and strung as double-basses.

---

* In the London Exhibition of 1851, a monster double-bass mounted with three strings, was shown by M. Vuillaume, who gave it the name of *Octo-bass*. This instrument was both more powerfu¹ and also descended several notes lower than the ordinary double-bass. The so-called *Pedal-bass* of the above-named M. Dubois, which war wrought forward at one of the subsequent Exhibitions in Paris, was intended as a substitute for the organ in the orchestra. See Gretchel's book, as above, p. 224.—*Tr.*

No. IV.

OF THE BOW.

Although the violins of Amati, Stradivarius, and others named in the third chapter of this work, are still regarded as the finest ever manufactured, the bows in use at the time the above makers flourished have justly given place to those of modern days. Indeed, from the time of Corelli to the present period, constant changes have been made in the form and increased length of the bow, until it has at last been brought—chiefly by the labours of Francis Tourte, of Paris—to the high state of perfection in which the violinist now finds it.*

The bow consists of the *stick*, into the upper part of which, called the *head*, one end of the *hair* is fastened by means of a small wooden plug. The other end of the hair is held by a projecting piece, termed the *nut*, which can be moved by means of the *screw* at the lower extremity of the stick, so as to enable the player to tighten or slacken the hair at pleasure.

For the violin, tenor, and violoncello, bows of a similar make are used, the chief difference being in the length and thickness of the stick. They are all furnished with white horse-hair, and, when loose, the nearest approach of the stick to the hair should be exactly in the middle, between the head and the nut.

The violin bow is about twenty-seven inches long, and

---

* See the drawings of bows in Plate 3 of Baillot's "*Art du Violon;*" or the interesting book of M. Fêtis, before-mentioned, on *Antonio Stradivari.*—*Tr.*

contains from 100 to 110 hairs.* The tenor bow only differs from it in having a somewhat thicker stick. The bow for the violoncello, besides having a thicker stick than either of those before named, is one or two inches shorter. The double-bass bow is shorter still, and has, of course, a thicker stick than that for the violoncello. It is made in a variety of forms, and supplied with black hair, as being much stronger than white.

Various kinds of wood are used for bow-sticks ; such as Brazil (or Fernambuc) wood, snake-wood, iron-wood, log-wood, &c. the best of which are the two first-named. The nut of the bow is generally made either of ebony or ivory.

Some of the finest modern bows are those made by the late J. B. Vuillaume, of Paris,† who has remedied two serious inconveniences under which they have laboured, as hitherto constructed : the first arising from the difficulty experienced in arranging the hair so as to form a perfectly even surface throughout its length ; and the second, from the nut constantly changing its position, which necessarily alters the length of the hair ; and hence the performer, who ought always to keep his thumb close to the nut, is obliged to place it at different distances from the head of the bow—which varies the length, and consequently the weight, of this part of the stick, and is sufficient to affect the extreme sensibility of touch which is in a manner transmitted from the hand of the performer to the extremity of the bow.

---

* This was the number formerly, but Abele says it is now from 175 to 250. See *Die Violine*, 2nd Edit., 1874, p. 156.—*Tr.*

† For full particulars of the bows of the celebrated F. Tourte, the reader is referred to the work of M. Fétis, on *Antonio Stradivari*, (English Edit., p. 109). In England, the bows formerly manufactured by John Dodd are highly esteemed.—*Tr.*

In the improved bows of Vuillaume, these inconveniences have been removed in the following manner :—the nut, which is of ebony, is hollowed out internally, and permanently fixed to the stick, and the hair is fastened to a kind of interior nut of brass, which, as in ordinary bows, is moved backwards or forwards by means of the screw.

It will be observed, on inspection, that the inner nut can be made to recede or advance by the requisite quantity, without the least variation in the length of that portion of the hair comprised between the head of the bow and the exterior nut.

The hair is firmly fixed to a kind of cylindrical nippers at each end, and the inner nut, together with the head of the bow, is pierced through to receive them; so that the performer himself can arrange the hair with the greatest facility, and likewise renew it whenever he desires.*

Steel bows have been invented by Vuillaume, which have met with the approbation of many of the first performers; but they are not likely to supersede those made of wood, to which, in general, the preference seems to be given.

---

* Another invention for this purpose is that of Mr. Walker, Aberdeenshire, which consists of two small metal hinges, fixed respectively to the head and the nut of the bow, to receive the ends of the hair.—*Tr.*

No. V.

OF MUTES AND FIDDLE-HOLDERS.

In order to subdue the tone of the violin, a small metal or wooden clip, shaped somewhat like a double three-pronged fork, is, as every player knows, placed occasionally on the bridge ; the three prong-like portions of the mute passing between the four strings, on each side of the bridge, and thereby clipping it firmly. The term *con sordino* directs the player to apply the mute, and *senza sordino* to remove it.

Complaint, however, having long been made of the inconvenience occasioned to the player, by the act either of applying or of removing the mute during performance, M. Vuillaume successfully overcame the difficulty, and, in 1867, brought forward his *Sourdine pédale*—or, as we call it in England, the *Chin-mute*—by means of which, and without the least interruption in the execution, the violinist is enabled, by the simple pressure of his chin upon the tailpiece, to bring the newly-designed mute into immediate contact with the bridge. The possibility of thus producing new and varied effects, both in orchestral music and in solos, will at once be obvious, and an additional charm will be thereby attained.

The difficulty of holding the violin in a firm and unconstrained manner with the chin, without bending down the head, so as to be able to pass the hand on the finger-board from one position to another, with perfect freedom, and at the same time without the danger of disturbing the instrument or the tranquillity of bowing, is so exceeding great, that the eminent violinist, L. Spohr, invented what he called a *fiddle-holder* ; which, on being fixed to the violin by a peg passed into the hole usually occupied by the button, not only supplies the purpose of this button, by receiving the string or wire of the tail-piece, but rises above the latter in a convenient manner to meet the player's chin ; which, resting upon *it*, and not as heretofore on the *belly* of the violin, leaves this most important part free to vibrate, and thus adds both to the quality and volume of the tone.

Another and more simple form of fiddle-holder was made for the celebrated performer, Wieniawski, by Mr. George Chanot, of London, which is readily fastened to the violin on the left side of the tail-piece, without disturbing any part of the instrument, and can be as readily removed. This, in fact, constitutes its great merit, and should commend itself to every violinist.

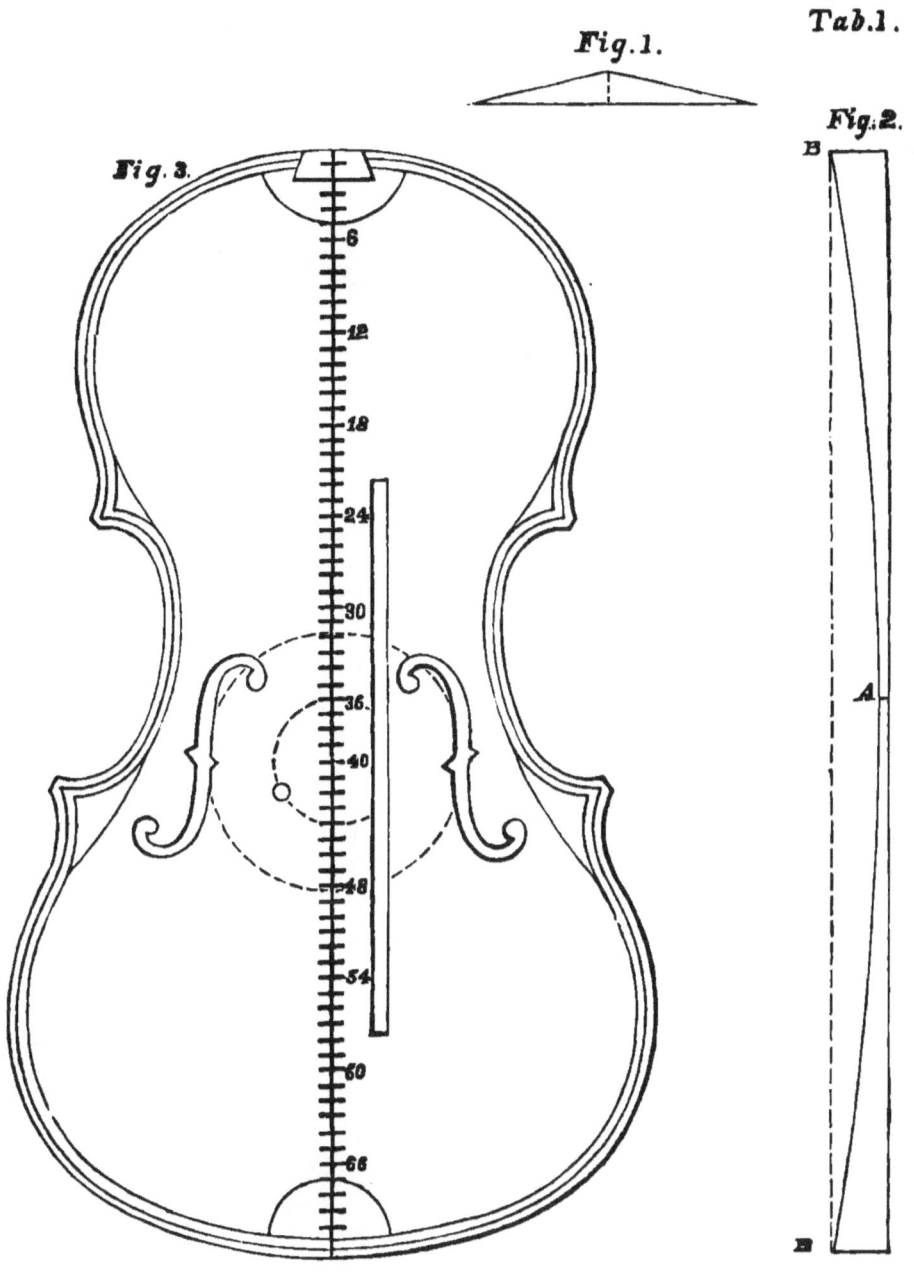

Fig.1.

Tab.1.

Fig.2.

Fig.3.

Tab II

I

C

D

Tab III

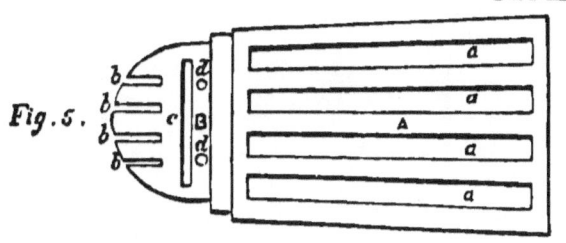

Fig. 5.

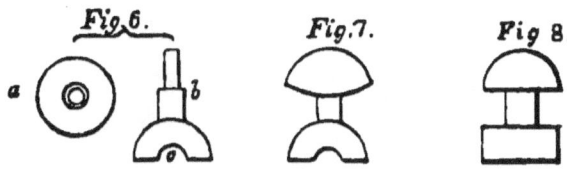

Fig. 6.   Fig. 7.   Fig 8.

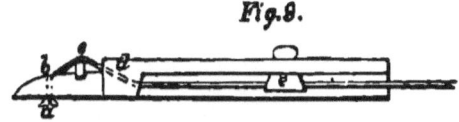

Fig. 9.

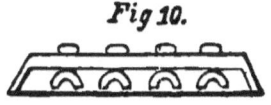

Fig 10.

GENERAL INDEX.

ı ʏ · ʏ - ' ˀ ͻ ͻ